KF.

My World in Motion

My World in Motion

Jo Whiley

Published by Virgin Books 2009

2 4 6 8 10 9 7 5 3 1

First published in Great Britain in 2009 by
Virgin Books
Random House, 20 Vauxhall Bridge Road,
London SW1V 2SA

www.virginbooks.com
www.rbooks.co.uk

Addresses for companies within The Random House Group Limited can be found at:
www.randomhouse.co.uk/offices.htm

The Random House Group Limited Reg. No. 954009

A CIP catalogue record for this book is available from the British Library

Hardback ISBN 9781905264766

The Random House Group Limited supports The Forest Stewardship Council [FSC], the leading international forest certification organisation. All our titles that are printed on Greenpeace-approved FSC-certified paper carry the FSC logo. Our paper procurement policy can be found at www.rbooks.co.uk/environment

Mixed Sources
Product group from well-managed
forests and other controlled sources
www.fsc.org Cert no. TT-COC-2139
© 1996 Forest Stewardship Council

FSC

Typeset in SwiftEF-Light by Palimpsest Book Production Limited,
Grangemouth, Stirlingshire

Printed and bound in Great Britain by
CPI Mackays, Chatham, Kent ME5 8TD

For my wonderful Grandma and Grandad for exemplifying everything that's good and great about being in love for a lifetime and for creating such a fantastic family to be a part of

My World in Motion

Sister

When my sister Frances turned forty last year, we threw a huge party for her. Mum told me and Dad that we were going to invite everyone – the whole village, all Frances's friends, all the people we'd known throughout her life. When Dad and I wondered why it was so important to throw a big bash for Frances Mum became incredibly agitated.

'Don't you see?' she said to us. 'It'll be Frances's wedding day.'

She was right, of course. We had to give Frances her own special day. Frances has meant so much to us. That's the case with each and every member of any family. But Frances is different from most people, and the difficulties Mum and Dad – and I – experienced because of that difference have shaped all of our lives and made us who we are, as individuals, and as a family.

Frances will never have a real wedding day because she suffers from *Cri du Chat* syndrome, a rare chromosomal disorder. It is characterised in babies by a mewling, cat's cry, hence its name. Frances has severe learning difficulties. She can read and write, after a fashion. She has friends, interests, is mad about music. But she'll never live by herself, never work, never have an adult relationship, never drive a car, never have children. She will for ever remain a child and so my parents' responsibilities to her – and mine, to a certain extent – will continue for as long we all live.

It was years before we were given a name for Frances's condition. She is three years younger than me, and for Mum and Dad, the realisation that Frances was not 'normal' was gradual. When she was six months old, Mum took Frances to a GP, who told her, almost casually, 'She's probably going to be spastic.' Mum remembers crying all the way home. In some ways I think it was a blessing that she didn't then know what lay ahead, how she and Dad would struggle to care for Frances. At eighteen months old Frances had a small epileptic fit and spent a night in hospital. Mum was called into a doctor's office, alone, and told that Frances was brain damaged, that she would never walk or talk properly, and that she would have severe learning disabilities. Then she was sent on her way. Mum simply took her home and got on with the business of working out how to bring her up.

At Frances's fortieth, Mum made a speech which had all of us, and me in particular, in floods of tears. She described how their lives had changed for ever when Frances was born, but she also underlined the extent to which she and Dad benefited from the kindness of others – neighbours, friends, health professionals, social workers, all of the people in the village. Having Frances drew them into a close-knit, loving community, something that many people go through life without these days. Frances was her usual gregarious self during that speech – she's such a complex character. If you didn't know her, you might think she wasn't listening. She sat at Mum's feet, seemingly in a world of her own, but every now and then she'd interject, at full volume, clap furiously, or race across and squeeze whoever had just been given a special mention, and it'd be clear that she was following what was being said intently. At one point Mum was referring to the fact that it'd been years before Frances had learned to speak, and Frances called out, 'WELL I CAN TALK NOW!' It was a moment of comic genius, brilliantly timed. At times I think she's far smarter than the rest of us.

Until I was about five, we lived in a tiny council house on Aberdare Road in Northampton. Mum often tells me that I was due on the 5th of June, but was born on the 4th of July, ten months after they married, and that even after she was finally induced I took forty-eight hours to be born. I'm not sure if that can be true, but, as Mum likes to say, it does seem to have set a pattern for the rest of my life. Dad was an electrician, working on building sites, Mum worked here and there doing odd jobs to make ends meet. My memories of those early years of my life are hazy, blurred at the edges, played out as if on a scratchy reel of celluloid, the home movie in my mind. Dad went off to work each morning armed with an enormous ghetto blaster, customised with his name – 'MART'S RADIO – KEEP OFF' – and 'COME ON YOU SPURS' in red sticky tape down the sides. It was a comical sight, I realise now, because Dad is not the tallest of men, and the ghetto blaster was always huge – they seemed to get bigger and bigger every year. If there's a DJ-ing gene, then I inherited it from Dad. I often think that he should've been an entertainer at Butlins or Pontins. In many ways, he's more of an extrovert than me – he loves being up on stage with a mike in his hand – relishing being before an audience. I struggle with it to this day, although I've grown used to it over the years. But Dad and I share a love of music and of playing it, loud, for others to hear – spreading the word.

We're musically evangelical, Dad and I. (I get sent CDs all the time, and I have to watch Dad like a hawk because he'll take a new CD of a major band home, which hasn't yet been released and which I have because the band is coming in to do the show. I'll discover the CD's missing and ring him in a panic – 'Dad, do you have the new U2 CD?' – and he'll confess that he's been playing it because he thinks it's so great.) My Dad has always had great ears for a hit record and spots the potential in so many bands way before they achieve success. Long before Elbow got their Brit and Mercury awards my Dad was telling anyone who'd listen how brilliant they were. Same with Kasabian, Dido – too many to mention.

There was always music on in the house when Dad was home, and he and I would sing along, belting out our favourite tracks –

Billy Joel, Sweet, Status Quo, David Essex, Gerry Rafferty, Carly Simon, Fleetwood Mac. He was a sucker for those quirky records that surprise everyone by becoming a number one hit – 'Nice One Cyril' and 'Always Look on the Bright Side of Life'. Any car ride turned into a massive sing-along – these days he does it with my kids, twice a day, on the school run. On the building site he was the life and soul, and that ghetto blaster would churn out the tunes for his fellow workers from dawn till dusk, he'd organise them into groups for sing-alongs and take requests. Today, the ghetto blaster has been replaced with an iPod, which is always stuffed with new tracks and a playlist for every conceivable occasion.

In that scratchy film in my mind, Dad heads off to work each morning in his overalls and hobnail boots and the house falls silent. Mum and I go about the business of our day, quietly, as if we – and the house – are biding our time, waiting for his return. Jerky images spring up when I try to recollect those daytime hours: wobbling around the cul-de-sac on my white mini push-bike (all the other kids had Raleighs, which I coveted), my skinny legs straining to turn the pedals; playing by myself in the back garden; helping Mum with the chores; trailing behind her down to the shops; listening to 'Listen with Mother' while eating boiled egg and solidiers. I remember watching only a little bit of TV – programmes such as *Hector's House*, *The Woodentops* and *The Herbs*, that lasted five minutes or so each.

Dad's return from work was momentous. He and the ghetto blaster would steam into the house, and the place would be humming again. He'd clean his fingers with vast quantities of acrid green, sticky goo and I'd stand on tiptoe next to him in the bathroom, transfixed. Then the music would be on – vinyl, the ghetto blaster was strictly for the sites. The tunes from those days are so vivid to me: The Platters, a fifties Black American crooning a cappella group I love to this day – I must've heard 'Smoke Gets in Your Eyes' a million times.

Mum and Dad were always very cool; Mum had such style and

dressed with panache – she stood out from the other mums in our street. She was a hair model and so her hair was always well cut and dyed and she kept it very short, which was unusual back then. She was seriously glamorous, never a dolly bird. (She worked in a dress shop for a while when I was little, and I sometimes wish I'd spent more time paying attention to the advice she gave her customers and less time lying on the changing room floor, eating crisps. If I had, maybe I wouldn't have made so many fashion faux pas along the way.) Ever the fundraiser, she organised dinner dances and barn dances, I used to love watching her get ready, lying on the bed as she painted her long nails and did her make-up. Dad's no stranger to the bleach bottle himself – basing his look on Robert Redford. He jacked the habit just a couple of years ago. We had a friend, Tony, who came to the house and did the whole family's hair. (Later, he was the only one who could cut Frances's hair. Tony would do this extraordinary routine, twirling about, dancing, singing, and every now and then lifting up a chunk of her hair – snip, snip – while she shrieked and took swipes at him. Then he'd whirl away again and do something to make her laugh. He was magical and he became very key in our lives. After Mum lost her baby at forty, Dad threw a dinner party for her, at which Tony leapt out of a huge cardboard box wearing a leopard-print thong and bow tie. It was the first time I'd seen her laugh in months.) Mum and Dad are a great partnership and always have been – especially on the dance floor. I can still see them, jiving to 'Jailhouse Rock' at the swimming club disco. The floor would clear as everyone watched in awe. As a fourteen year old with two left feet, I'd stand watching in the corner, mortified. It's only now that I can look back with pride.

An annual event in the Whiley calendar was the Sidmouth Folk Festival. I think it was the closest we got to taking a holiday without Frances in those early years. Dad would be clad head to toe in cheesecloth and denim and platforms – I think he really appreciated the era of the platform shoe, since they added a good three inches to his height. I remember sitting there in a pub, listening to someone playing a really beautiful song. Mum has always been a massive Elvis fan – while Dad would listen to anything and everything Mum remained faithful to the King. I'll never forget on our family holiday in Great Yarmouth going to get the morning papers which proclaimed 'The King is Dead'. I ran back to our caravan in a state of excitement yelling 'Mummy, Elvis is dead!' and seeing her world crash around her as she heard the news. A lot of folk music takes place in pubs where singers gather round and take turns to sing shanties and ballads. Just pure, beautiful voices unaccompanied by instruments ringing out to a mesmerised audience, pints in hand. I'm sure this is where my love of a good voice and acoustic music (or singer-songwriters) comes from.

Dad was a massive Spurs fan and we'd sing 'Ozzie's Dream' whenever his team were playing. (He's still a huge fan; he and Mum live in a really picturesque village, in a gorgeous cottage – a little wooden gate, pansies in the front garden, path up to the freshly painted front door, and then a huge poster in the front window: 'Come On You Spurs', not the effect Mum is looking for, I suspect.) In 1981 he took me to the FA Cup Final, Spurs against Manchester City. Ricky Villa and Ozzie Ardiles were playing at the time. I was in my teens by then, but I'd never been to Wembley and it was my first gig experience, a taste of something truly marvellous to come. We stood there on the terraces, screaming out that song as the huge crowd roared all around us. I remember it so vividly – the hair on the back of my neck standing up, the excitement, that unique sense of a collective experience, of a thousand voices becoming one. I think I've been a festival girl since that very moment.

Life happens so fast that the memories get lost along the way. We moved when I was about five to a brand-new estate, brand-new house, all very 1970s and idyllic – we lived on Pheasant Way. I don't remember Frances's birth. She's just there in that jerky home movie from a certain point, at my side with her thick, coke-bottle glasses and her funny, stumpy boots that were supposed to help her walk. I don't remember a moment when I recognised that she wasn't like the other kids, although from very early on I was fiercely protective of her. I just always knew she was different – there were endless trips to the doctor, and we shopped for her shoes and glasses in 'special' shops. But she was my little sister, my sidekick. She crawled until she was well over three and didn't stand up and walk until she was four. Even when she did finally walk she was knock-kneed, tiny and spindly, so she looked quite unsteady on her feet. In those early memories she is mute – she didn't start to make sounds until quite late, grunting sounds and squawks and certain sounds for simple words like 'hello'. When we were very young she was in a silent world, but she and I communicated perfectly; we were close in the way that only sisters can be.

There was so much drama in our lives because of Frances. As she became more mobile she grew incredibly accident-prone. She has no sense of danger, and she isn't terribly coordinated. I'd walk home by myself from school, as children did back then. As I approached our front door I'd call out to Mum, wondering whether they'd be home. Sometimes I'd push open the door and there'd be blood all over the floor, neither Mum nor Frances would be there, and I'd know to go next door to the neighbour, to wait until they got back from the hospital. Frances was energetic, fearless and adventurous. She loves her food and once the floor was awash with blood because she'd licked the jagged edge of a can of apple sauce and cut her tongue open. Mum would get us both dressed up to go out and then, just as we were leaving, we'd realise that Frances had disappeared and we'd find her sitting in the paddling pool. We had a climbing frame in the garden and one time she dodged outside when Mum's back was turned, climbed it, crashed to the ground, and returned to the kitchen, all in the space of a minute or two, with the bone sticking out of her elbow. I remember Mum and I frozen, staring in horror, and then it was all hands on deck as usual, the crisis routine we all knew so well – me round to the neighbour, Mum bandaging the arm as best she could and bundling Frances into another neighbour's car. She broke countless other bones over the years. She was also in and out of hospital when I was young to have operations to help her physical problems – eye operations to help correct her sight, for example. I'd be sent off to stay with my grandparents for days while she and Mum were away, something I loved rather than resented. My grandparents were wonderful people, instilling a strong sense of family, supporting my Mum and Dad through the crises but always calm, unflappable, warm and loving. My Grandma turns ninety this year and is a formidable woman – just beautiful inside and out.

Frances suffered from fits, and there was a wooden spoon in the kitchen with cloth wrapped around it, which Mum would put into her mouth to stop her from swallowing her tongue. I remember coming home and seeing Mum holding Frances as she jerked and shook. What strikes me most about that memory is Mum's expression as she held her convulsing child. I am not exaggerating when I say that she was always calm, implacable; she never panicked. And she was totally accepting of the situation that she and Dad had found themselves in. I have no recollection of either of them seeming to despair, to ask, 'Why us?', I think a lot of that is down to Mum's strong Christian faith, but also her solid nature.

Children are amazingly resilient and accepting of their circumstances; I don't remember being afraid for Frances, or upset when she had fits or injured herself. It was just what happened. I accepted the fact that they had to go off to the hospital regularly because of some drama or another, and it never occurred to me that Frances might not come back. I was never frightened, never fully aware of the danger she put herself in. The accidents were just part of the fabric of our lives.

I can see Frances crying, with rage and frustration. She

seemed to cry so often. She had the most stupendous tantrums, toddler tantrums which grew stronger and wilder the older she became – by the time she was ten or so they were terrible, violent and physical. She would lash out at us, smash anything she could get her hands on. She was very strong by then, a huge force. There was absolutely no way of getting her to do something she didn't want to do. She'd literally be kicking and screaming, no matter where we were – she is to this day completely uninhibited. The noise would be stupendous as she lay on the floor in a shop or in the street, drumming her feet and yelling. Mum was never ruffled, was always calm and resolute, but Dad – and I – sometimes struggled with it. It was so hard not to be furious with her. You'd have a plan, a day in the countryside, a trip to see something, and then Frances would refuse and there would be no point in trying to reason with her. If you tried to force her, things would just get worse. Over the years we got used to simply letting her have her own way for the sake of peace and our collective sanity. I still marvel at the way my parents handled Frances. They never once, in all those years, lost it with her, were never physical, never hit her. They must've been under such enormous stress and pressure and yet they were, outwardly at least, calm and loving with Frances, with me and – perhaps most extraordinary – with each other. You hear so often of couples splitting up under the strain of having a child like Frances.

We were really cloistered on our estate. It was a proper community and everyone there pulled their weight around Mum and Dad and sheltered us from some of the worst aspects of having a child with learning disabilities. A neighbour could always be relied upon to look out for me when Mum and Dad were dealing with Frances. There was no need for explanations, people accepted Frances and took her into their lives. We always played out in the street with the other kids. I remember sensing the difference when we went out into the world – I hated people noticing Frances and would become incredibly fierce, staring down anyone who looked at her for too long, holding their gaze until finally they looked away, embarrassed.

The hardest thing to cope with was the fact that Frances didn't sleep – a common characteristic of people with *Cri du Chat*. She barely needed any sleep at all when she was young, and Mum and Dad tried everything. I can see endless teams of experts coming in to try this and that therapy, each specialist convinced that they'd be the one to crack the problem and that it was some failing on our part that led to her sleeplessness. Time after time they'd leave in the morning, utterly defeated by a night trying to quell Frances. Medication only made her more hyperactive – she seemed to fight against sedation. We were told to remove all distractions from her bedroom. The bed was nailed to the floor, because as Frances got older she became incredibly strong – she has the constitution of an ox – and she'd overturn it, smash it up. The curtains were attached with Velcro so that they could be taken down at night so she couldn't destroy them. There was nothing else in her room. Mum and Dad were told to settle her for the night and then shut her in and that she'd gradually relax, so she had a sort of gate across the door. Needless to say, nothing worked. On one occasion Frances was quiet, seemingly for hours, but when Mum went to check on her, she discovered that she'd torn her entire mattress to shreds with her bare hands.

My parents would take turns trying to get her off to sleep and as I grew older, I would try to help as well. I'd lie there in bed and listen to the drama unfolding – Mum and Dad downstairs, trying to watch TV, the howls of protest from Frances getting louder and louder, one or other parent coming up to sleep with her, and then as the night wore on, that parent becoming more and more despairing. At some point I'd feel I had to go and take a turn, too, or she'd lie there shouting for me until I gave in and went to her. I'd lie down with her, telling her stories for hours on end to keep her quiet, until finally I'd drop off only to be woken by a clout to the head with Frances saying 'not asleep are you Joanne?' We all grew adept at telling stories and snoozing at the same time – 'Goldilocks' was a particular favourite – a trick that has stood me in good stead as a parent. After what seemed like hours, she'd sign to me that she wanted Daddy now, and in he'd stumble as I headed for some precious shut-eye. Another night, another game of musical beds. And often, in desperation, when I felt I'd go mad if I had to run through the little bears' breakfasts one more time, we'd lie there and she'd play records – I can still hear Perry Como's 'Magic Moments', played over and over until the first light of dawn. We listened to the radio together all the time as well, we both loved it. Every weekend we'd have Ed Stewart on and sing along to all the songs on the Junior Choice show – 'Nelly the Elephant' and 'Ernie the Fastest Milkman in the West', the two of us lying on Mum and Dad's bed. We were waiting to hear our names called out, because Mum had written in and requested a song for us. I don't remember hearing the song, just the pleasure of lying there with my flame-haired sister, who was squeaking with delight and jiggling up and down on the bed. The radio played such a key role in my childhood. I even loved being ill and staying in my parents' bed, listening to Jimmy Young. I always found it so comforting: that familiar voice was incredibly soothing, and created such a feeling of intimacy; lying there, cosseted, I'd feel as though I was included in his world. Being ill was marvellous, because I could doze off whenever I wanted, free of the guilt of knowing that someone else was with Frances. TV never held the same appeal as radio and we didn't watch it that often – when we did, it was usually a family activity – TV at teatime, and we'd all watch together.

When Frances was about eight, the family went to see a play about Helen Keller. Mum came away filled with inspiration. 'Since Frances may never learn to speak, we'll teach her to sign,' she said. Mum had been desperate to find a way to communicate with Frances, and knew she could recognise all her letters and numbers, but there was no known sign language for people with learning disabilities. Mum went on a course aimed at helping parents to teach children to sign and, in the end, partly devised her own system: thumbs together for 'Daddy', hands clasped for 'Mummy', index fingers curled together for 'Johanne' (me). Once she'd grasped these signs we added more and then, to our amazement, Frances began to vocalise, make grunts and sounds for things, and then gradually to utter words. It was like a miracle. Later, when she went into residential care, her speech improved further and, by the time she was twelve, she was able to speak. Now it's perfectly easy to understand most of what she says, although she has damaged vocal chords, meaning that her voice is extremely deep and she has trouble modulating it – she can only speak very loudly. Without quite understanding how, Mum is certain that mastering sign language unlocked a door in Frances's mind that led to her mastering speech. It's hard to describe what a difference this made for her and for all of us. We were suddenly more aware of her as a person, she was able to communicate with people outside the family, and she was less frustrated. I imagine that these days she'd have been given speech therapy fairly early on.

When a couple have children, they become a tribe – Steve and I have spent the last seventeen years creating the Whiley-Morton tribe. There's a sense, when you have your first baby, that you've set yourselves together as a couple, shielded from the outside world. I think the moment when I was born must have been incredibly important for my dad, because he didn't really have a family of his own. His mum left home when he was four or five. When he was about eleven Dad contracted TB from his father and spent a year in a sanatorium. His rheumatoid arthritis is a legacy from that period of terrible illness. He hadn't been home for very long when his father was hospitalised and soon died. He went to live with his grandfather, Pap, but Pap worked at night, so from six each evening Dad would be left to his own devices.

Often he'd climb out of a window and roam the city streets, getting into all manner of scrapes. His grandfather died when Dad was fourteen, and from then on he was completely alone in the world. He got an apprenticeship as an electrician and that was that. He rarely talks about his childhood. Working on this book has made me realise how little I know about him and his family, but such a beginning can only have had a profound effect on him. Yet Dad is blessed with an incredibly sunny nature; he's the most gentle, loving man, and he'd never complain about the hand life dealt him. I think that when he met Mum and they married and had me, he was rescued from the feelings of loneliness he must've felt so strongly. Mum's family couldn't have been more different: close-knit, loving, pillars of the community. In her, Dad found the family he hadn't had as a child. He told me once that he'd had a younger sister who died as a toddler and also an aunt who was 'a bit funny'.

My childhood wasn't normal, then, but the older I get the more I wonder exactly what a normal childhood is. Certainly, having Frances made life pretty difficult, and I was always aware of that. Teenage rebellion just wasn't an option for me – I knew I could never do that to Mum and Dad. We could never go on holidays, as Frances would become terribly agitated if she was taken out of her routine. Once a year we'd try it – we visited a place called Hayling Island on the south coast, where The Spastic Society, as it was then called, had a bungalow. More often than not, it'd end in disaster. Frances would be thrown by being out of her natural environment. She didn't really like the beach. We'd take turns; a couple of us would be down on the seafront while one of us was inside the house, playing music for Frances. I remember sitting facing the sea with Mum. Dad would streak out of the house bearing a tray, gin and tonic for Mum, and a soft drink for me, hand them over, then whisk back to the house before Frances had noticed he'd gone. Often we'd come home early, exhausted, defeated, I think all three of us thinking, 'never again'. It was as though the place was jinxed – I remember being the sickest I think I've ever been there, staggering back from a sea walk, puking into every bin along the esplanade. Steve came once, early on in our relationship (confirming his saintliness to me once again), and lost his car keys on the beach. We spent hours hunting for them until the RAC came to our rescue and broke into the car. But at some level I think it always did us good to be away, out of the usual routine. Our options were very limited anyway, since there wasn't a lot of spare cash, and in any case there was no hope of getting Frances on to an aeroplane. And so Mum and Dad would decide each year to give it another go. There were moments of pleasure among the horrors – including countless games of Bingo, slot machines and miniature train rides – Frances loved riding on the model trains they had there. I think the fact that they persevered says an awful lot about the way they chose to bring up Frances. They did their absolute best to maintain something akin to normal family life; they let Frances be herself. They didn't just take the easier way with her, which would've involved being far more rigid and controlling, and they always included her as a member of the family. And while none of it was easy, I think it was better for all of us to have lived like that with her. Steve always says that Frances is the person she is because Mum and Dad treated her like a person rather than a problem, and allowed her to express herself and to develop her personality. And he's right, as he is so often.

These days, Frances is so much happier and calmer. Mum and Dad took her on a plane last year, for the very first time. Some friends from the village took them all to Portugal. In spite of everyone's misgivings, it passed off just fine. Frances spent hours by the pool, apparently, watching the others having fun in the water. It felt like the most enormous breakthrough, and Mum and Dad came home jubilant. Steve lost a lot of money over that trip – he was convinced it'd be a disaster. He and I had a bet, and I won. Not that I didn't have my doubts, but I'm an optimist at heart, and in any case I felt that I had to put my money on Team Whiley pulling it off.

When I was thirteen we moved out of Northampton, to Great Brington, on the Althorp Estate, home to Earl Spencer, brother of Diana, Princess of Wales. Part of the reason for the move was that Frances's tantrums were at their peak then and I think Mum and Dad wanted a little more space between them and their nearest neighbours. They took over running the shop and post office in the village. We lived upstairs and Mum worked in the shop. It made their life so much easier, and I sometimes wonder how they would've survived if we'd stayed in Northampton.

I struggled a bit with the move, as any teenager would. I had to change schools, leaving behind a smallish middle school and starting at Campion School, which was by comparison huge – it was a big 1970s comprehensive. I was a bit lost at that school; I was one of those children the teachers never seemed to notice. (I still get emails from people, telling me they were in my class at school, although they can't remember me at all – 'But well done anyway.') Certainly I never spoke up in class and didn't really ever involve myself in activities, apart from swimming and the other sport my PE teacher thought I was suited for: shot-put, which presumably has to do with my broad shoulders and large feet.

The school bus would pick me up each morning from right outside the shop, but somehow I was always late – the habits of a lifetime begin early. I'm not sure what I'd be doing, but the bus would arrive and I'd realise I wasn't even dressed. At least twice a week I'd miss it, even though it was parked literally outside the front door. It drove Mum mad. And it's obviously genetic, because my daughter India does the same thing today.

By then I was swimming competitively, something I'd been doing since I was eleven, and the swimming club provided my social life and gave me a sense of belonging. It saved me from being miserable at school. It's a great thing for a teenager to do – it keeps you out of trouble as you're way too tired, most of the time, to get into mischief. Often in those days we'd have all been up most of the night, on and off, taking turns with Frances, until at about four or five in the morning she'd finally drop off to sleep. Five days a week Dad would then get up at 5 a.m. to take me to swim training. How Dad survived on so little sleep and then put in a day on the building sites, I do not know. I remember days when I'd be so tired myself that I'd be more or less asleep on my feet as I staggered to the pool. I always seemed to reek of chlorine and the pool complex was far from glamorous – I'd swim into a fresh batch of drowned cockroaches each morning. But I loved it, and I always felt great after the swim. I am, needless to say, really good at getting by on not much sleep, provided I can exercise.

The swimming club was wonderful for the whole family. I can picture us all there while I trained, Mum sitting on the edge of the pool, practising her sign language as I ploughed up and down for hours on end. I'd be able to sign from the water – 'How much longer?' or 'Get me a drink.' It was very handy. Mum and Dad made lots of friends among the other long-suffering parents, and the discos were one of the highlights of our social calendar. We'd listen to all the music I still love today: Earth, Wind and Fire, Kool & the Gang, Evelyn King, Sylvester, Jocelyn Brown's yearning, poignant 'Somebody Else's Guy'. And, of course, the song that was always played at the end of the evening, The Commodores' 'Three Times a Lady'. How many times did I stand there, making a pact with God, in the desperate hope that someone would ask me to dance? He never did come through for me. Those were the last days of disco, I was thirteen years old and I desprately wanted to go see a film with my friends but my Dad put his foot down. In my memory the film was *Saturday Night Fever* but when writing this I checked with my Dad who insists it was in fact *The Stud* . . .

Our friends at the club knew and accepted Frances. She was a regular feature at galas, a fully participating member of the audience. As I've said, Frances has an extraordinarily loud, deep voice.

She'd be in the stands, with Mum and Dad, watching me at some swimming meeting (I was county champion three years running, and swam pretty seriously until I was fifteen, when boys and teenage life got in the way). There I'd be, poolside, my permed hair tinged green from all the chlorine. 'Ready, steady . . .' the starter would call. I'd bend forward on the starting block. And then, 'GO!' Frances would shout, her voice bellowing out like a fog horn. I can't recall how many false starts she caused, but there was no keeping her quiet. Thankfully no one ever suggested that it might be better if she stayed outside during the races.

Back then, Frances was desperate to swim like me, and she once took part in a special gala. She was tenacious and brave, and she managed a whole length, backstroke while, in a reversal of roles, I cheered her on from the stands. I can still see her now, this tiny creature, legs dangling down, arms straining behind her, giving it everything she had. We were all immensely proud of her.

My late teens seemed to pass by in a whirl – I have few distinct memories, more a sense of the mood of the times. By then I'd made lots of friends, and life seemed to involve hours spent hanging out, gossiping, talking about bands and listening to music. We were a tight group of friends, boys and girls. There were lots of gigs to go to in Milton Keynes, which was regarded as a national joke even back then, with its concrete cows and jungle of roundabouts, but most big acts played at the Milton Keynes Bowl, and I was often in the audience, as close to the stage as I could get. David Bowie, REM, The Police – I saw as many of them as I could. My long-suffering Dad replaced early mornings at the pool with late nights, driving a group of us to gigs, waiting for us all, and then driving us back home. It's only now that I realise how much he'd have liked to be asked to come and watch with us – he goes to gigs as often as he can these days.

I had a dear friend called Noel, who fancied not me but Barbara, my considerably bustier, prettier friend, but Noel and I were inseparable. He was incredibly sporty, and though he didn't drive – none of us did – he cycled everywhere on his beloved bike. He lived about twenty miles away, but he'd cycle over most week-ends. One day he turned up with his new racing bike – he was so proud of it. We headed out to take it for a spin, and I decided I'd give it a try. I whizzed down the hill, near Althorp, while he was shouting instructions – 'Don't take your feet off the pedals; Don't brake too suddenly; Don't change gear! Lean into the corner!' I was going faster and faster, out of control and terrified, but doing as I was told. Then I hit the corner, didn't lean in, went straight ahead and over the handlebars. I lay there, gasping in agony, but mostly feeling horrified by the sight of Noel's beloved bike, which was lying next to me, a mangled mass of rubber and metal. Noel flagged down an old man driving a white van and we bumped and jiggled back over every painful cattle grid to my place. The pain was excruciating – I'd broken my collarbone – but all I could think about were the months Noel had spent saving up for that bike. But because he was my bestest friend, he wouldn't hear a word of apology.

Playlist – The teenage years:

The great tracks from that time are still so vivid to me. Each one seems to evoke a thousand memories:

U2, 'I Will Follow' – I can picture a bunch of cool upper-sixth-formers telling me that they were off to see U2, when I was still in the year below. I had no one to go with, just wasn't in their league, and yet I was deeply envious at the thought of hearing this song played live. They were the arty crowd and seemed so bohemian and cool, everything I wished I was. They were living a life that seemed so much more exciting that mine. The part of me that will for ever be a shy, gawky girl from Great Brington, still can't quite believe that I've interviewed U2 many times, and had them in the Live Lounge earlier this year.

Thompson Twins, 'We Are Detective' – this band represents one of those wrong turnings you make in your life and look back on with deep regret. I had the choice of seeing The Smiths or the Thompson Twins. I chose the latter, without really knowing why – it probably had to do with who was going to see them. It was a mistake I swore I'd never make twice.

The Clash, 'White Riot' – my moment of revelation, when I discovered the joy and excitement of seeing a band live, was at Bingley Hall, in Birmingham, my first ever gig. I'd never heard The Clash before that night, but I've been a fan ever since.

The Human League, 'The Sound of the Crowd' – I vividly remember the performance of this on *TOTP* – Phil Oakey and his unfeasibly lopsided fringe and the intensity of the song. Just brilliant. I knew, then and there, that I wanted to be part of that scene.

David Bowie, 'China Girl' – I remember being at a party with all of my friends. It was in the days when *The Tube* would do video exclusives and everyone would stop whatever they were doing to watch. We turned the music off and stood around to watch and then this extraordinary, sexy love song came on. She was so beautiful, both song and video were totally captivating.

Although I was there, it's hard even for me to imagine what it must've been like for Mum and Dad to have brought up Frances. Their lives were totally given over to caring for her – and they still are, and they always will be. For those of you who have children or know a little child well, think of the intensity of looking after a toddler – the tantrums, the falls, the constant attention they demand. Then imagine what'd be like if that toddler grew to the size of a large adult, but retained all of that toddler behaviour, combined with immense strength, occasionally violent, and an inability to sleep at night. But alongside the stress and difficulty is the joy that being with a small child can bring – the affection, the unrestrained, crazy behaviour, the hilarity. I remember hours and hours of romping with her, tickling her, making her laugh, her unbridled affection and warmth. These things were the flipside of the tantrums, the sleeplessness, the accidents. And Mum clearly wanted more children. One of the moments of my childhood that I remember with complete clarity is lying in bed in the attic at my grandparents' house when I was eight or so, waiting excitedly for the news that my new baby brother or sister had been born. Dad appeared, knelt by my bed and told me that Jesus had taken the little baby to live with him in heaven. (Years later I learned that the baby had been stillborn.) After that I remember nothing more but, to this day, the memory evokes a profound sadness.

Then, when Mum was forty, I was twenty, and Frances seventeen, Mum became pregnant again. By that time, genetic testing was available. Mum went through the agonising period that I've been through four times now, waiting to hear whether the baby had a genetic abnormality. They learnt two devastating things on the day the tests came back: that Frances was diagnosed with a disorder named *Cri du Chat* and that so did their unborn fourth child. I was at college in Brighton by then, and had gone on an exchange trip to France. I've never felt so alone and so far away from home. I remember Mum telling me that she was pregnant. I was completely surprised, and then I was overjoyed. Then, when I rang again some weeks later, Mum told me that the baby suffered from Frances's condition and that she'd had a termination. I was devastated. Of course, she must have been more so, but she didn't let on. That's not her way. By then she was very involved in her church, which is evangelical Christian, and that must've made her decision all the more difficult. The day I learned about the termination, my friends and I went to see the musical *Cabaret* in which Liza Minelli's character, Sally Bowles, has a termination. By the end of the film I was inconsolable and for days felt bereft. So sad for my Mum, her loss and for what might have been. It was one of those moments you experience on the threshold of adulthood, a sense of the end of innocence, the loss of that assumption that life is on your side, that things will always be OK. I'm well aware that Dad went through that passage to adulthood earlier than any person should, when he was effectively orphaned at a very young age. What Dad learned the day he and Mum got the tests back was that he was the carrier of *Cri du Chat*, which explains the sister who didn't live past infancy, and the aunt who was 'a bit funny'. He and I have never spoken about any of this, but now that I'm a parent I can begin to imagine what he must feel about it. Later on, I was tested and discovered that I too am a carrier of *Cri du Chat*. And I've handed it on to my children – India and Cass, but not Jude and Coco, so when they come to have children they too will have to have them tested. I've been so lucky in that my four children are not affected by the condition although, as a carrier, the odds of my producing a child with *Cri du Chat* are quite high – one in ten. I've never had to make the agonising decision Mum made with that last pregnancy.

The upside of learning about *Cri du Chat* was that we now had a name to give to Frances's condition. Shortly after this, Mum and I took Frances to a weekend away organised by the *Cri du Chat* support group. I think we all felt that we'd finally get to meet other people who had children like Frances, that there'd be a chance to compare notes and tips and even make friends. Mum and Dad benefited enormously from friendships with the parents of children with learning disabilities at the schools Frances attended, but we didn't know anyone with a child quite like Frances. We came away from that weekend disappointed. We know why this is – Frances's condition is what's known as a 'trisomy', which is a certain type of genetic mutation, so although she shares many of the characteristics typical of the syndrome – the inability to sleep, lack of speech and temper tantrums – she is in many ways quite different. Frances's behaviour seems more consistent with severe autism, but is difficult to define – she's one of a kind. Back then, it was a case of going on doing what we'd always done with her: figuring out what worked best for her, and for us.

When she was about eight – around the time we moved to Great Brington – Frances began to be sent away to residential schools, with varying degrees of success.

The first school Frances attended was called Beech Tree House, near Cambridge. Mum and Dad received funding for Frances to be there from the Northampton Education Board. Anyone with a child in residential care will know the trauma of the goodbyes punctuated by fighting, wails and screams, followed by the silent, guilt-ridden driven home. But Beech Tree House was a wonderful place, run by two incredible people, Malcolm and Nina – they were amazing with her. There was still a great deal of drama, tantrums, refusing to sleep. She'd smash her room up at night, make herself sick, wet herself – anything to get attention. She ended up once again in a room pared back to a single bed bolted to the floor. One night Frances pushed herself out of a tiny window, high up the wall (no one could work out how she'd climbed up to it), leaped two floors to the ground below, shattering her hip and arm, before astounding her carers watching TV downstairs by limping into the room and requesting a cup of tea. In the end, they came up with the most brilliant way of keeping her happy. She had a ghetto blaster, which, like Dad's, was her most treasured possession. One of the carers customised it so that it took tokens to play songs. If Frances was good, cooperative, and stayed in her room all night without problems, she received tokens so that she could amuse herself for hours on end playing tracks. If she was naughty or uncooperative, she lost a token. It was a highly sophisticated form of star chart, and sometimes it worked.

From Beech Tree House, Frances moved to a place nearer home, in Wellingborough, and would come home at weekends. Then, between the ages of twenty and thirty-four, she lived in a residential home in Bedfordshire. There she was taught to garden, sew and cook – skills which might help her to be self-sufficient. This is the place I remember the most clearly. She was happy there, although she did sometimes try to run away. On occasion the police would be called when she ran away, or the fire brigade called when she set off the fire alarm.

Things came to a head when this place was closed and Frances moved again, to a newish institution, run privately for profit. Mum and Dad noticed that Frances seemed to be growing increasingly distressed and that the staff didn't seem adequately qualified to deal with her. There were signs that she was being heavily medicated. She was running away more and more often. Then she came home one weekend covered in bruises, I think because they'd been restraining her, and that was that. There was no way Mum and Dad were going to send her back. So, for the past six years, she's lived at home with them. She helped out in the shop for years, until Mum retired and she and Dad moved to a bungalow nearby. Frances has government funding, which pays for her to spend some days at a day centre. None of us quite know what will happen to Frances in the future, because she will always need twenty-four-hour care.

My husband Steve has been wonderful with Frances from the word go, and I'm so grateful to him for it. He treats her in the same way he would any other person. He's larger than life, sociable, and very loud – and so he and my sister have a lot in common. I think I knew for certain that Steve was the one for me when he first stayed with Mum and Dad. I was living down in London by then and we came up for the weekend. We had a truly terrible night with Frances. She is always distressed by storms, and that night there was a huge one, with thunder and lightning, guaranteed to set her off. It was a very long night. I lost it and shouted at her, there was screaming, doors slam-ming. By dawn we had given up on bed and were sitting around the kitchen table, three of us exhausted and unable to speak, the fourth chatting away happily. At about nine Steve strolled into the kitchen, looking surprisingly fresh and perky. 'How did you sleep?' I asked nervously. 'Great, thanks,' he answered, and then, 'Why, what happened?' when he saw the look of utter incredulity on all of our faces. The man can truly sleep like a log; he hadn't even stirred with Frances standing over him, bellowing in his ear. One thing I think people find hard to understand is the extent to which we feel blessed by Frances. She is funny, loving, warm, intense. Everybody who meets her adores her. She doesn't see the world like we do, and there's an enormous freedom associated with having someone around you who doesn't comply with societal norms. We weren't a family obsessed with material wealth and we sure as hell never wondered what other people thought of us – not much hope of keeping up with the Joneses with Frances in tow. Any Whiley family outing could descend into mayhem at the drop of a hat – Frances deciding to remove her clothes if they felt tight, lying shrieking on the ground in a supermarket, opening the door of a car moving at speed, clearing a restaurant table with one swipe and sending everything crashing to the floor, one or other of us completely losing our rag with her. We've seen and done it all with Frances. It gave me an odd freedom as a teenager too. I was a bit of a loner at school, but I was so protective of Frances that I was in some ways sheltered from all the usual teenage anxieties. There was an unspoken sense that if you weren't with us Whileys as a tribe, then fine, well and good. We sure as hell weren't going to try to win you over.

Zoom forward a few years in the jerky images from my memory and there are Frances and I, out together on our regular jaunt. I'm thirteen or so, freshly permed and tinged faintly green as always. Fashion hasn't occurred to me yet (it didn't really until I became a public figure and had it more or less forced on me). I'm a skinny girl who thinks wearing odd socks exemplifies personal freedom and the right to self-expression. Frances has two-inch-thick glasses on and her funny little boots – she was working an emo look thirty years ahead of her time, like Velma from *Scooby Doo*. We set off each Saturday morning, just the two of us, getting the bus into Northhampton, where we head straight to the record department of Beattie's. Each week, we buy a vinyl seven-inch – she's been music-obsessed for years now. Frances always knows exactly what she wants and will have been monitoring the charts all week. (To this day, we all have to guess what will be number one and the countdown is always an emotional roller coaster – joy if Frances's favourite track makes it to the winning slot, despair if it doesn't. She has a book in which she records the family's guesses each week. Several dead relatives and pets are included on the list, and they go on getting a turn each week, too.) Once we've flipped through the albums and listened to a few tracks, we make our purchase before setting off to the nearest tea shop, where we treat ourselves to a nice cup of tea and a slice of cake. Then, back at the station, we make for the photo booth and take a series of snaps of the two of us, cheek to cheek, before boarding the bus for home. It's a weekend ritual that lasts for years.

Because my mother is a fighter, from early on she got involved in projects associated with people with learning disabilities. When we were living in Northampton she perceived a lack in the availability of specialist toys to help people like Frances, and so she helped create a toy library. I loved it – I remember playing on the outsized tricycles. There was a massive red barrel which we were allowed to have for the week if no one else had taken it out. I'd be there all day helping Mum, praying no one would want it. If we did get to have it I'd put Frances inside and roll her along and she'd laugh as she bumped round and round.

Perhaps Mum's greatest achievement has been setting up the Rocking Roadrunner Club in Northampton. We are all painfully aware of how little there is for Frances and her friends to do – other than the day centres, there's really no opportunity for them to get together and socialise. And it's a mistake to think that they don't want to. Frances is an extrovert – she and Dad are round at the pub most nights, and she's got a number of people in the village she visits regularly. Frances develops crushes on people which are incredibly intense and obsessive. At the moment she is very keen on Jacqui, who runs the pub. Frances heckled Mum quite a bit during her speech at her fortieth, interjecting in that trumpeting bass of hers. At one point she bellowed, full blast, 'I'm going to MARRY Jacqui.' Fortunately Jacqui sees the funny side of Frances's infatuation.

Frances and many of her friends are mad about music, so Mum has created a club night, which is held four times a year. It's one huge, fabulous party. Frances and I DJ as the Whiley Sisters, although mostly Frances doesn't let me near the decks. She knows exactly what to play – she'll put on Scissor Sisters and the whole crowd will start throwing these amazing shapes. There are some great characters who are regulars. There's Justin, who has Down's. He's always smartly dressed in a pressed white shirt and tie. He has his own idiosyncratic dance routine: a series of forward rolls, then furious air guitar, followed by more forward rolls. It really works. I took Coco along recently when she was a newborn. They were so tender and loving with her. One man came up to say hello, looked at Coco and then snatched her before I realised what he was doing. Thankfully he just gave her a kiss and handed her back. My kids love the Rocking Roadrunner. And Dad, well it brings out his inner Butlins Entertainer man, big time. It's hard to get the mike out of his hand. It's Frances's finest hour. And we all have Mum to thank for it.

She's a doer, not a campaigner. She's had the most wonderful, poignant letters from parents describing how their (adult) child had spent all day getting dressed, putting on make-up and jewellery, and how they'd had the best night of their lives. In fact the first night out of their lives.

When people ask me what it was like growing up with Frances,I often surprise them with my answer. It was, I tell them, incredibly funny. She's hilarious, Frances, sometimes intentionally, sometimes not. There's something enchanting – and liberating – about her total lack of inhibition. When Princess Diana died, Mum took Frances down to watch the funeral cortège bring her body home to Althorp to be buried. Frances is a big girl these days and not terribly mobile, so Mum had her in a wheelchair. She was immediately ushered to the front of the throng lining the road. Mum knows just how unpredictable Frances can be – if something confuses her or she feels upset, she'll have these outbursts of raw emotion, incredibly powerful, and intense and vocal – and so she tried to hang back, but well-meaning people kept pushing her forward. Steve and I were at home (everyone remembers where they were that day), watching the whole thing on the news, with the rest of the nation. We have this added dimension to the Diana story, of course, because Mum worked in the Great Brington shop all those years and sold Diana memorabilia and Diana even came in a few times. So we all feel that we knew her just a little bit. Steve and I were glued to the television, watching it with India. 'Look, there's your Mum and Frances,' Steve said. And there they were, on our screen, at the front of the crowd gathered at the gates to Althorp. The *Sky News* presenter continued his colloquy about the sombre mood, the car bearing the coffin turning into the gates, the crowd pressing forward. That total hush that I don't think I've experienced before or since. The whole country fell silent that day. And then, in the midst of that utter stillness, a voice I knew so well: Frances. 'GOODBYE, DIANA, GOODBYE,' she shouted, leaping out of the wheelchair, clapping furiously, cheering, but wailing at the same time, because on one level she knew Diana was dead. It was her personal tribute to the people's princess, beamed out around the globe. Later, when we'd stopped laughing, Steve and I watched the next round of the *Sky News* bulletin and noted that Frances had been carefully edited out of the footage of Diana's body making its final journey.

*   *   *

It's because of Frances that I agreed to become an ambassador for Mencap, the charity for people with learning disabilities. They initially approached me with the idea of organising a big concert in aid of the charity, but somehow that didn't feel right. Then they suggested organising a series of acoustic gigs at the Union Chapel in Islington, London, and I said straightaway that I'd be involved – how could I refuse? It's like getting to organise my own mini-Glastonbury. The Union Chapel is exquisite, very ordinary from the outside, but ornate within, with beautifully carved pews and an arched ceiling that seems to curve up to the sky. It's awe-inspiring and yet intimate at the same time. The idea was to get various bands to play short sets over a number of nights. When they came to me they'd already had some interest from various acts, but once I'd thought about it I decided that I'd get out my address book and pull a few favours. I figured I'd give every act to whom I had some close connection a try, and that one or two might say yes. But the response was extraordinary. I wanted to mix up established acts with some new faces, and I was trying to think who it'd be interesting to see doing something acoustic. That first year, 2006, we had Kasabian, Mika, The Kooks, The Fratellis, Amy Winehouse, Lily Allen and – my two biggest coups that year – Chris Martin from Coldplay and Noel Gallagher. It was as if Chris Martin and the Union Chapel were made for one another – that pure, fragile voice of his in that echoing space. Noel came on alone and did his first ever acoustic set, something he later told me he'd always wanted to do, and he was just amazing. You can see for yourself – his gig's on YouTube.

I had ten whole nights away from home, which was terribly exciting. I'd planned to catch up on more than a decade's worth of sleep, but late-night drinking sessions with the acts kept getting in the way – by the end of it I was yearning to be back with the kids and Steve, watching *Deal or No Deal* (I'm a sucker for Noel Edmonds) and having a cup of tea. I managed to race back to Northhampton once, to the usual chorus of, 'When are we going to see more of you, Mummy?' To which I answered, 'Next week!' and the chorused response was, 'But you said that two weeks ago!'

Amy Winehouse nearly gave me heart failure by being incredibly late. She didn't rehearse, just pulled up minutes before she was due to go on stage. 'It's OK, she runs on Amy time,' her people kept telling me. And she was fabulous. Lily Allen walked out on stage and announced to the crowd that her parents were married in the Union Chapel, which was a great moment.

It's a unique thing, playing in that space, and I think the bigger the act, the more they feel it. The first row of pews is just a foot or so from the stage, which is so low you can step down off it (or, if you're Johnny Borrell from Razorlight, step out from it on to the pews and into the audience). The audience can see the whites of your eyes. The lighting is beautiful – they put tea lights around the balcony – but there's no camouflage. It's acoustic, so there's no masking your playing or your voice. It represents the unmasking of an act, and that's why it's so remarkable that so many great musicians have agreed to do it. Mostly they're terribly nervous before they go on. I'll never forget Mika having a religious moment – in the vestibule, waiting to go out on stage and praying, eyes raised to the heavens, hands folded together in supplication. Then he went out and blew everyone away.

There was such a great response to the first year that we decided that we'd chance our arm and make it an annual event and, so far, we've done three years. (And I have tricks up my sleeve for this November, too.) That second year, 2007, I had the anxiety of seeing whether I could repeat my address book trick. I decided to aim very high, and so I sent Bono a text which read: 'Urgently required: rockstars for Mencap gig.' I half hoped that they'd do it because Edge has a niece with learning disabilities. Their response was non-committal: 'We'll see what we can do.' I was on tenterhooks. But, in the end, Bono and Edge said they'd come and do something. We decided to keep it a secret. That night Liam Fray, the lead singer of The Courteeners, was going to do a solo performance. We announced that there would be special guests and then I had to tell Liam that U2 were going on before them . . . The poor thing took it very well and well and truly held his own later that night. I came out to introduce Bono and Edge, saying we had some newcomers tonight, Paul and Dave, who were really nervous. The audience reaction was just fabulous – shrieks of amazement and delight as they realised what they were seeing. It was great to hear them both – Edge has a lovely voice, too – singing unaccompanied in the chapel. I'm so grateful to them. Bono was totally charming about doing it, telling a journalist later, 'When Jo calls, you come.' Not true, of course – rather the other way round – but really sweet of him to say so.

So many other bands played that year: Biffy Clyro, Johnny Borrell and drummer Andy Burrows from Razorlight (who came back again for me last year), Snow Patrol, Adele (who also came back for me last year), Duffy. The Little Noise Sessions are something I'm really proud of doing, and I hope to be able to keep organising them for years to come. It'd be nice to think that they'll become a feature of the London music scene, and that the bands – brand-new and established – will keep on wanting to play for Mencap.

When Snow Patrol played last year, Leona Lewis had done a session in the Live Lounge on my show and had covered their song 'Run'. It'd caused a bit of a furore among Snow Patrol fans, as is often the case – and I have to say I'm a fan of the original in this case – anyway Snow Patrol, to this day, insist they've never heard her cover, and when they came out on stage that night, I asked singer Gary Lightbody if they'd had a chance to listen to it. No, they hadn't, he answered politely. 'Well,' I said, 'I've got a special surprise for you tonight. Leona has agreed to come along and I'm going to bring her out now to duet with you.' I managed to say it with a straight face. Gary froze, a look of undisguised horror on his face, as he whirled around to look for Leona. 'Only joking!' I told him. The rest of the band collapsed in hysterical laughter. I'd really got him. They tease him about it to this day.

I took Frances to one of the Sessions the first year. I was anxious about it, because the acoustics in the chapel are extraordinary – you can hear a pin drop. Frances's voice does carry, and as I've said, she has a low boredom threshold. Sure enough, halfway through Jamie T's set, the audience are still and rapt when Frances calls out: 'ARE THEY FINISHED YET?'

What was wonderful about Frances's fortieth is the sense that Frances has touched so many people's lives. She's not only special to her family. She's a real feature of village life, whether it's from the days when she was behind the counter at the shop, or parked on the bench outside, greeting each customer as they went in. These days she's down the pub with Dad most evenings, and spends long afternoons doing her rounds – pottering round the village making visits, managing just like Winnie the Pooh to turn up at the right moment for 'a spot of something' – in her case tea and cake. She's loving and caring, especially with older people, and when she gives you a hug you feel as though you've received a gift. On the day before her party, the sight of the entire village clubbing together to put up the marquee, decorate it and prepare the food, was extraordinary. She had three hundred of her closest friends there that day – teachers from her schools, people from the days of the swimming club, even the woman who used to sell her records at Beattie's. Frances has the sort of social life and loyal friends a lot of people would envy. Of course, a huge part of this has to do with people's admiration and fondness for Mum and Dad, my amazing parents, who've been so strong and brave and optimistic all these years.

When I was about eight, Dad gave me a reel-to-reel recorder he'd got from somewhere, and Frances and I would play at recording our voices, me talking DJ-style, introducing tracks, interviewing Frances. I'd say, 'Hello, Frances,' and she'd grunt an answer; she loved making sounds to be played back to her. Then I'd put on a record and she'd dance, Frances-style, wiggling it for all she was worth. Showtime! If I've said that when I'm in the studio at Radio 1 I'm talking to a fictional audience of one, rather than the hundreds of thousands of listeners actually out there on any given day, then I think that person, my audience, has and always will be, my little sister, Frances.

Here is Frances's track list, songs she's always loved, tracks she plays when she's DJing because she knows they'll get her audience out on the floor.

Playlist – Frances:

Flying Pickets, 'Only You' – the song that had to be sung to Frances at my wedding, over and over, to get her to be a good bridesmaid.

Dead or Alive, 'You Spin Me Round (Like a Record)' – no disco night is complete without this track.

Frankie Goes to Hollywood, 'Relax' – needs no explanation. Another disco classic.

Madness, 'It Must Be Love' – Frances always dances to this with her head down, hands on the floor, bottom in the air, wiggling it like crazy.

Black Lace, 'Agadoo' – I have such a strong reaction to this song. Ordinarily, I'd be like most people and shriek 'Turn it off!' But I associate it with car rides when we were young. Frances was always so unpredictable in the car. If she suddenly felt bored, anything might happen. She's still like that today, you have to keep her singing and clapping or she might suddenly try to open the car door or grab the steering wheel. Back then she was a lot, lot worse. And she was mad for 'Agadoo'. So I remember hurtling down the road in the car, trying to tune out 'Agadoo' as it blared out of the stereo for the tenth time in a row.

ABBA, 'Dancing Queen' – that's what she is, Frances, a dancing queen. (I don't know anyone who doesn't like a bit of ABBA, and Frances is mad for it.)

Tony Christie, '(Is This the Way to) Amarillo' – another staple of any of Frances's DJing sessions.

Village People, 'YMCA' – Frances can do the hand movements and everything.

Dexy's Midnight Runners, 'Come On Eileen' – 'Play the Eileen song again!' I can still hear Frances shouting that. God knows how many times she and I danced to that track.

The Proclaimers, 'I'm Gonna Be (500 miles)' – another favourite Chez Whiley. Frances used to belt it out at the top of her lungs.

Status Quo, 'Rockin' All Over the World' – my Dad has an unhealthy obsession with the Quo and Frances shares his love for this track.

Donny Osmond, 'Puppy Love' – Pretty much her all time favourite.

Cliff Richards, 'Congratulations' – when we did a top ten at Frances's fortieth, this was number one, because we're all so proud of her.

DJ

Working on this book has forced me to organise fragmented memories into some sort of narrative. When I look back over my life, the memories seem to swirl around and rise up as though from the Pensieve – the magical, rune-strewn bowl in the Harry Potter books in which fragments of memory are stored. If you're going to tell the world your story, then you'd better settle down and try to work out what happened and why. I've tried to isolate the big moments for me, the defining, life-changing ones. The biggest are obvious: meeting Steve for the first time and knowing that he was 'the one' – just knowing it with absolute certainty. That might sound like a cliché, but it's how it happened. The birth of each of my four children, all that pain and intensity and exhaustion, and then the moment of pure joy when the little creature was laid on my chest and looked up at me as if to say: 'Ah, there you are, Mummy, finally.' I have welcomed each of my children into the world with a flood of pure love and I know Steve has felt the same way.

I think it's relatively rare to experience a moment when you feel quite certain about what you want to do with your life. It's much more common to fall into a career, more a case of feeling your way than making a conscious choice. Artists have it, I guess, a moment when they recognise in themselves a burning desire, a need even, to act or paint or write or make beautiful music. I'm not suggesting that wanting to be a DJ represents the discovery of an artistic vocation. But the moment when I knew that I wanted to work in the world of music, and probably on the radio, was a dazzling ray of sunlight at the end of a bleak time in my life.

I'd struggled through a course at Brighton Polytechnic, with a boyfriend who was a deeply unhappy person, totally wrong for me. It's no coincidence that it was my goth period. It suited my mood. Memories of sitting in a basement, wearing black while everyone watched horror films and smoked dope (I hated both) come flooding back whenever I think of Brighton, and I have no desire to go back to that dark place. As well as being a committed goth, the boyfriend was a massive Jimi Hendrix fan; Hendrix was the first thing he played in the morning, the last thing he played at night. Because of that, and despite the fact that Hendrix is a musical genius, I still can't listen to him – it's amazing how evocative musical memories are. There are hilarious memories from that time too, mostly associated with the goth look. The uniform of the goth was, of course, black, black and more black. Occasionally purple was allowed, but only if worn with black leather and lace. The make-up was severe – heavy on the kohl eyeliner – the lips were crimson and the hair was just colossal. Anyone who's ever dabbled on the dark side will know a goth's best friend are their crimpers. My hair had been permed for years; now I'd spray an entire can of hairspray on it and then apply the crimping iron in a vain attempt to get it to stand up. After a few nights out, the fried gunk on my crimpers would be set hard, and I'd have to spend hours chipping it off in order to fry my hair once more. At some level I felt like I was in fancy dress the whole time, I felt a bit wrong and depressed and crap. But those years of late adolescence are intense and often difficult for everyone, and for this reason evoke really vivid memories. I look at India now and know that she's on the threshold of making that big leap into the adult world and my heart aches for her.

Playlist – the goth years:

The Cult, 'Spirit Walker' – one of the bands I saw play in Brighton. They were so exciting, just beyond brilliant. The singer, Ian Astbury, was the most extraordinary-looking man; lithe, gorgeous and an amazing dresser. I saw them because of my moody, sulky goth boyfriend but in many ways they were the antithesis of him – vital and full of energy.

The Sisters of Mercy, 'Alice' – there are so many tracks to choose from, but I think that this is their defining one. Although goth music reminds me of dark times, I genuinely loved the music, and I think this track sums up what was great about it. A number of the members of The Sisters of Mercy went on to form The Mission – with whom I made my first, slightly disastrous, foray into interviewing.

Bauhaus, 'Bela Lugosi's Dead' – I was always so proud because the band were from Northampton. I'd be working in Wallis as a teenager and I'd see these incredibly cool people, all dyed hair and skiny jeans, walking past the shop, and I'd know that I was looking at the band or one of their entourage. At college, whenever I told someone I was from Northampton they'd mention Bauhaus and I'd feel a tiny bit cool, just by association. God, I'm sad.

New Model Army, 'Vengeance' – I think possibly one of the reasons this music appealed was because of the dancing. It's well-documented that I can't dance and goth music required no dancing at all, just a moody stare and lots of shoving – all elbows and DMs. The only dance I could get away with.

I'd chosen to study Applied Languages at Brighton Poly. French and English Literature were my strongest subjects and I'd always assumed that I'd become a speech therapist. I'd witnessed first-hand how frustrating it is to be denied the power of speech and I'd seen Frances's joy as she'd finally learnt to communicate through language. But the course was not at all what I was expecting – I was the first in the family to go to university and we were naïve, to say the least, about what to expect and how to select a college, and my marks hadn't been great in the end, so my choices were more limited than they might've been. The course was beyond esoteric: it was all about how language is created, its physical components – syntax, semantics, phonetics, linguistics. We learned Russian so that we could experience what it was like to come to grips with a new alphabet. I was utterly out of my depth, I loved language and literature, but this was mathematical and logical. I think I understood about ten per cent of what they were teaching me, and none of that was Russian. Although I do remember how to say 'I love you', so if I ever meet a tall, dark, handsome Russian, it might well have been worth the misery. In another life I'd have switched courses or quit, but without hindsight I just muddled through. It wasn't the first time. I once did work experience while at school with a speech-occupational therapy unit. They'd made scones with raisins in. Now, raisins are to me what kryptonite is to Superman. I cannot stand them. However, because I also don't like offending people, I ate the whole scone, complete with dead bluebottles. With every mouthful I got the sweats, and I started gagging, like Paul Burrell eating a kangaroo's testicle. In the end, I had to excuse myself to the loos where I promptly threw the whole lot up.

Towards the end of the course I finally split up with the goth boyfriend and put Spear of Destiny and New Model Army behind me, and things began to improve. I made a wonderful group of friends, many of whom I'm still in contact with.

And then, when the time was ripe, when I was happy and confident again, that defining moment, that shaft of sunlight. One of my college lecturers was asking me what I wanted to do with my life. I told him I had no idea, but that I loved music and I was fascinated by radio. So he suggested that I volunteer for

Radio Sussex. At first, I was horrified by the idea. I'd never been outgoing at school; I was never a performer and I was always too shy to put myself forward. But every now and then I'd be picked to read something – a poem, say – and I'd be really happy, because I loved using my voice. As a child I'd watch *Jackanory* and fantasise about reading stories to the nation. A little later, when I was a teenager, my first Saturday job was in the dress shop Wallis. The place would be heaving with middle-aged ladies who shopped to the sand of muzak. Until I took control of the sound-track to their shopping, that is. I just couldn't resist it – playing Heaven 17's '(We Don't Need This) Fascist Groove Thang' and thinking I was being *so* subversive.

So, once I got it into my head, the idea of DJing was very appealing. I knew that I liked to play music to people, and no one would be able to see me; I'd be hidden away. The radio programme was called *Turn It Up*, it was a local radio show which aired on a Sunday night. It was a complete misfit – stuck between the farming news and religious programming on a Sunday night. Basically, anyone who wanted to could go along and get involved – doing interviews and, ultimately, becoming one of their pool of presenters. A radical music free-for- all show.

There's a photo of me which I love, because it marks that defining moment for me. I'm wearing headphones for the very first time, behind a desk, beaming up at the camera, the biggest smile on my face. I look so happy and relaxed and free. I knew, without a doubt, when I put on those headphones and spoke into the mike for the first time that I wanted to be a DJ. I loved every-thing about it – the adrenalin hitting a few minutes before you were about to go live, finding bands I wanted to play, thinking of how to introduce them. It was peculiar how different I'd become when I got behind that mike – not tongue-tied, not shy. I'd be off. The words would fly out of my mouth. My spell on *Turn It Up* was really my education and coming-of-age; all the angst of that Brighton period was worth it for that brief time on-air. I remember a fellow DJ suggesting we play Screamin' Jay Hawkins on the show. We'd never even heard of him, but within ten seconds of listening, we were hooked – and it's been that gut reaction, that primal instinct, that I still have now when I listen to a great new track and decide I'm going to get them on the show. It was a great crowd at the station, a group of people with amazingly diverse musical tastes, all feeding off one another's passions. It taught me how important it is to be open to listening to new material, how pointless it is to be a musical snob. I'd arrived at *Turn It Up* thinking the only music was goth music, but I left with a new love of hip hop, blues, dance, indie – it was here that my eyes were truly opened.

I discovered the joy of interviewing bands, too. Again, some sort of mysterious alchemy took place and I found that I wasn't lost for words. My first was with goth band The Mission, which I was especially equipped for; they were a throwback to my days of student gloom, and I was secretly thrilled to be meeting my panto goth heroes. However, my first interview was a classic. Probably not the most probing interview they've ever done, but I went away feeling pretty smug until I pressed replay on the uher to hear nothing but a silent hiss because I'd made the classic journalist's error. I'd failed to hit the 'record' button. I had to trudge back, tail between my legs, and do the interview all over again. The band very sweetly ground through the whole thing for a second time. And I remember playing Laibach on the show – another hangover from my goth days, but their cover of The Beatles' song 'Across the Universe' is superb. I was discovering how interesting a cover can be; it teaches you so much about both the original band and the covering band.

Playlist – the Brighton years:

Primal Scream, 'Velocity Girl' – I fell in love with this wonderful, jingly-jangly pop song, nothing like the music that the band is known for today.

The Housemartins, 'Happy Hour' – gloriously upbeat, which summed up my mood as I discovered radio and a new life through *Turn It Up* – plus Norman was a Brighton boy so I'd sometimes see him about town. Through Zoe I've got to know him and he's the loveliest man and surprisingly shy. If/when I get to heaven, I want Norman Cook to be on the decks.

James, 'Sit Down' – a joyful anthem that makes me smile. James were one of the key bands on *Turn It Up*. After all those years in the land of the goth, they seemed wonderfully bright and shiny and uplifting.

You never forget to hit 'record' twice and so, in a way, it was lucky that I made that mistake at my very first interview. But technical difficulties befall all broadcasters. I'll never forget an encounter with U2, many years later. It wasn't the first time I'd interviewed them, but this was a massive deal. They'd specifically asked for me to come to Dublin, which I was thrilled about. We decided to make it into a special show, which would be broadcast around the world, to 145 million people, live. It involved going to their HQ, Hanover Studios on the banks of the Liffey. I was doing the *Lunchtime Social* on Radio 1 by then. Needless to say, I was nervous about it. My producer at the time, Pat Connor, was a huge U2 fan and she'd researched like you wouldn't believe – if she'd gone on *Mastermind* with them as her subject, she'd have cleaned up. I'd listened to everything they'd ever put out and read pages and pages of her research. In fact, I could've done *Mastermind* on them too (but would have lost on General Knowledge). We got there and they arrived, punctual as always. They're terribly professional and always gentlemen, but they have that rock star sheen which, to a novice broadcaster, makes them terrifying – or it did back then. These days I'm used to their company, but they are stellar. And there they were, sitting before me in a row, like an interview panel, sunglasses on, expectant. I zoomed through my introduction, the usual stuff about being poised to chat with the biggest rock 'n' roll band on the planet. Then the engineer began drawing his finger across his throat and gesticulating wildly. We'd lost our link to the outside world. We sat there grinning at one another for a bit. Larry Mullen shifted in his chair. Although it's Bono and The Edge you mostly hear about, Larry Mullen is the one by whom you gauge the mood of the band. He's very much in command, very careful about what the band do and when and how. So when he began to tap his foot gently, I felt the panic rise. The engineers were running about wildly, shouting to one another. I broke out in a sweat. Then Bono got up. 'Right, that's it,' he said, and walked out. Oh fuck. Bono had headed off, probably for home. This was truly a monumental cock-up. But the rest of the band remained sitting there calmly. I mumbled something lame about how it'd probably all be OK in a minute. Silence. Then the door opened and there was Bono, holding a bottle of vodka in one hand and a bottle of Jack Daniels in the other. 'What's your poison?' he asked me, plonking them down on the table. The relief! He was right of course; it was the only way to deal with the whole hideous scenario. We drank our way steadily through the hour or so that ensued and then right through the interview, which was probably much better for it. What nerves? I was the most chilled out I've ever been on air by the time we got our link up again.

Vocation firmly established, at the end of my time in Brighton, I heard about a journalism course at City University in London, applied and, to my delight, was accepted. The course was invaluable in terms of learning all the technical stuff, although a lot of it didn't really relate to what I was by then determined to do. You could see who was going to end up doing what – some of the students would be busy making documentaries and working in the editing suite; I'd be there, day in, day out, playing records and mixing and fiddling about with the decks. But we had a go at doing everything, and I knew I was heading in the right direction. After a while, I got fed up with commuting up and down from Northampton and moved in above a pub across the road from the college. Ironic really, because we lived next door to a pub in Northampton (Dad and Frances's HQ), and now I was literally inside one. It was a mad place. I remember being woken from a cider-induced stupor one night by a police raid. The land-lady was a piece of work, a marvellous Babs Windsor type; we might've been on the set of *EastEnders*. My weight ballooned rather with all the booze – until I got salmonella seriously hideous but it sorted out the weight gain, in any case!

Those were such great times when I look back on them. I felt as though I'd come into my own. The odd socks of my teenage years, the awkward gawkiness, feeling a misfit, were a thing of the past. I'd made lots of great friends. There was a trip to a Greek island and a night of moonlit skinny dipping with a Canadian waiter – it has to be done once in your life, doesn't it? My *Mamma Mia!* moment. There was the course, which was great. I was also listening to great music. What's my top track from those days? I think it'd have to be The Blow Monkeys, 'It Doesn't Have to Be This Way'.

These were definitely the days of being resourceful – I had very little money, being a student, and I remember getting up before anyone else to pick up the pennies from the floor to pay for my lunch each day. I say, 'pick up the pennies', really I was peeling the gummy 5p coins from the beer-soaked pub carpet before shoving them in my pockets. While I was living above the pub I was not alone – I had a little furry friend for company – Hammy the hamster – a leftover from my goth boyfriend. He should have been called Hammy Houdini after the great escapologist. Hammy did that hamster thing of disappearing one day (how *do* they get out – can hamsters bend bars? I think so.) and he remained missing for two weeks, by which time I'd assumed he was in Hammy heaven, only for him to reappear between the jaws of the pub cat; slightly punctured but valiant and fit to live another day

It's documented that I went to City University, but what is not so well known is that I didn't actually pass the radio journalism post-grad diploma, but came away with a big fat 'F' due to my failure to get to grips with law and shorthand. Fortunately I'd managed to make some good contacts whilst on work placements and thankfully they were willing to take a chance on me. Out of what could have been a negative came a positive: the person who ultimately failed me was my tyrant of an Arts teacher who became one of my very best friends: David Roper.

My first job was on a project called *The Radio 4 Generation*, which involved discovering what the youth of that time felt about the seven deadly sins (something I'd been doing my own personal research into above the pub). I'd go around the country – Bath, Birmingham, Liverpool – interviewing young people about their views on politics, contemporary culture, sex, health and social issues. John Humphrys later presented the programmes to critical acclaim. I loved it, loved all the travel, loved hearing what all these people were listening to, what they worried about. It laid the groundwork for my subsequent career – without realising it, I was making a connection with people who would be my audience in years to come.

The next stop was as a researcher on *WPFM*, a BBC Radio 4 youth culture and music programme that was broadcast on a separate frequency in the afternoons on what was known as 'Schools Radio'. The audience was tiny, but it was brilliantly produced, quite groundbreaking, and highly regarded as radical radio. I was in heaven. After a few years working as a researcher on *WPFM*, I was offered the job as presenter, taking over from Terry Christian and Gary Cowley. I was finally behind the mike. And I was listening to dance music for the first time since my days as Northampton's disco queen.

Playlist – the *WPFM* years:

Bomb the Bass, 'Beat Dis' – I'll always associate this track with my first years in the world of music. We had Tim Simenon on *WPFM*, but I'd first heard 'Beat Dis' when I was living above the pub and listening to John Peel one night while I was studying. He played the track and it was a Road to Damascus moment, such a new and exciting sound, completely cutting-edge. By the time I was at *WPFM*, it had crossed over completely and become a huge hit.

The Beatmasters and Cookie Crew, 'Rock Da House' – I loved the video; shots of Felix the Cat, edited to make him move to the beat.

MARRS, 'Pump Up The Volume' – a million miles away from Sisters of Mercy and The Cult, and part of a dance music revolution.

Eric B. & Rakim, 'Paid in Full' – we used part of this track as the theme music for the show and so whenever I hear it, I feel the adrenalin rush of being live on or with the show about to begin.

My next career move was sideways, into television, but it was hilarious and riotous. I worked briefly on a short-lived show called *Club X* on Channel 4, the most chaotic thing I've ever done – ninety minutes of live TV, which attempted to marry the arts and music and youth culture. *Club X* was a precursor to *The Word*, but it was far more unwieldy and dangerous – I booked bands for this before *The Word* – from the Jesus and Mary Chain to Happy Mondays to Imagination – literally anything went. I got the job after sending out a ton of letters to production companies. The only one who got back to me was Charlie Parsons – a whirling dervish of ideas and creative energy. When you worked for Charlie you surrendered your life for him and the show. I came in on a Saturday once because we were short of an idea for the show. My parents were coming to pick me up to go on holiday. Charlie told me I couldn't go on holiday until I'd come up with an idea so I told Mum and Dad they'd have to go without me! It paid off though, because

Charlie went on to give me my break with *The Word* and treated me so well.

It was less of a TV show and more of a freak show – week in, week out, there were shocks in store – East End gangsters and gay rights campaigners sharing the studio, and ultimately a man wielding a gun live on air. I used to take refuge with a fellow researcher, Danielle Lux, scared for our jobs if a feature didn't work and for our lives too, at times. My next brief stint was as a researcher on BSkyB's Power Station, which was set up as a music channel with the aim of rivalling MTV. Anyone out there remember the squarial? I was producing a three-hour weekly chat show called *Blue Radio*, presented by Boy George. We were trying to do terribly ambitious things, but it was produced on a tiny budget and the set looked as though it'd been put together on *Blue Peter*. Boy George had overcome his drug addiction by this point, and alternative therapies were very much the focus. It was a case of 'welcome to the inside of George's head' – we'd have Reiki healers and people from the Hare Krishna movement. But because of George's profile, we had some extraordinary guests: Spike Milligan on with a psychic one week, Mary Whitehouse and an expert on transcendental meditation the next. I spent a lot of time making placatory phone calls – to Spike Milligan's wife; to Mary Whitehouse, who was one of the crossest women I've ever met. We had live music, too – Lulu came on and sang 'The Man Who Sold the World'. And, in one of the greatest moments from my early working years, Jocelyn Brown sang 'Somebody Else's Guy', that track I'd danced to so often, alone beneath the silver ball at the swimming club disco. I felt as though I'd died and gone to heaven. I remember Poly Styrene from punk band X-Ray Spex agreeing to come in, but unfortunately she was in the throes of a nervous breakdown. A car was sent to pick her up, but she wouldn't come out of the house, so I phoned her and tried to talk her into opening the door, while she was having a full-blown delusional panic attack.

Each week I'd be convinced that the show was going to be a disaster and somehow it would all hang together in a very surreal sort of a way. George was the king of chaos. He'd have a stream of taxis waiting for him, for hours, while he fiddled about doing this and that. I'd be trailing around after him, trying to get him to leave for wherever it was he was supposed to be, or give me an answer on something. I adored him and we got on famously, but he was incredibly tempestuous. He's a big, solid bloke and he'd fly into rages, calming himself down by punching the filing cabinet, which grew more and more battered and wobbly. Sadly, Power Station was axed because not enough punters brought the 'squarial' needed to tune in. One song in particular provides the soundtrack to those mad days on *Blue Radio* though: Sinead O'Connor's haunting 'Nothing Compares 2 U', written for her by Prince.

Playlist – the Power Station years:

SNAP, '1 got the Power' – this was a signature Power Station video. Not necessarily a track I love but one I associate with my time there because it was on such heavy rotation.

Sinead O'Connor, 'Nothing Compares 2 U' – I'd loved Siinead's voice and music from the beginning. She was mesmerising – vulnerable yet fiercely defensive and was always making headlines for her controversial statements. This was a simple yet stunning video. Just her face with enormous eyes with a single tear rolling down her face at the end.

Adamski, 'Killer' – this was an early discovery. Adamski came into the studios to be interviewed along with his friend, who sang on the single 'Seal'. Both were very shy, bit awkward – really sweet. And it was such a monstrously catchy song.

It was while I was working at Power Station that I met Steve. Steve was a music plugger, who worked with New Order and other bands I loved signed to 4AD Records. At the time, he was plugging the wonderful 'World in Motion'. For months, we didn't meet, but we were on the phone all the time and we'd end up chatting about bands and gossiping. I thought he was someone I knew vaguely who was incredibly short with blond spiky hair. He was warm and funny, but genuine and down-to-earth at the same time. He never made me feel shy. Finally we met, at a gig at the club Subterranea. I'd gone to see Ned's Atomic Dustbin and Steve and I were introduced by a friend of mine. I remember looking at this tall, really good-looking man with long dark hair and startling blue-green eyes with orange at the centre – I call them jaffa eyes – and managing to squeak, 'Hello.' I clocked that we were both wearing the same silky blue bomber jackets – just in different shades of blue – it was a good omen. So he wasn't the short-arse with the bad hair after all! It was love at first sight – just like that gut reaction I have when I hear a great track. I just knew. Thankfully, he felt the same way. Something was up. As we were leaving, my friend told me he had a girlfriend, but within just a few weeks Steve rang to tell me that he was on the platform at Watford Station. He'd split up with his girlfriend and would I go out on a date? We agreed to meet at a pub at the end of my street in Notting Hill. I only had to walk two hundred metres or so, but I was still about forty-five minutes late. Steve likes to say that this pretty much set the tone for our relationship. Punctuality isn't my strong suit – I was about forty-five minutes late for our wedding, too. Steve's late Grandmother, Bella, was particularly pleased when I failed to show up promptly at the church as she thought I'd stood Steve up, and she was awfully fond of his former girlfriend, my predecessor. Her face fell when I did finally arrive. It was one of those golden summers that seemed to go on for ever. England was doing well in the European cup. We sat up night after night, listening to Van Morrison, drinking cheap Freixnet, a Spanish champagne, playing a lot of backgammon and eating chips and omelettes. I remember taking him to meet my parents and being relieved and elated when they all got on famously; Frances took to him straight away and Steve didn't bat an eyelid, he treated her as warmly and kindly as he would anyone else.

The first time Steve proposed to me, we were lying in bed and he said, 'If I whisked you away to a desert island, would you marry me?' No, was my answer, I couldn't get married without my family and friends. Steve likes to say that was a sign – he married four of us, not just one. Fortunately he wasn't put off and asked again, a little while later, and this time I said 'yes'. We told my parents on New Year's Eve that same year. The idea was that at the stroke of midnight I would pull my Dad over, Steve my Mum, and we'd tell them both at the same time in a nice romantic gesture. There's a photo of us all in the pub that night. Mum and Dad look overjoyed, but the most striking thing about the picture is the state of Steve and me. We're so in love that we're very round and chipmunk-cheeked. We planned to marry the following summer, which gave us time to hit the gym and work off that loved-up weight. We got married in 1991, about a year after we'd first met. And nine months and one day after that, we had India. I'm a terrible procrastinator, but when it came to Steve, there was no mucking about, nothing to think about.

Our relationship works on so many levels. Steve is my rock; he's the solid, pragmatic one. He's funny and clever and kind. He knows how to talk me down, and how to make me laugh. He's a wonderful father. He's also part of the world of music, which has worked so well for us. He often refers to himself as 'Mr Whiley' – very much like Cate Blanchett's husband who describes himself as 'the hand', because there'll be a shot of Cate at a red carpet event, and it'll be cropped so all that's left of him is a hand on her waist or her shoulder. In fact, if ever we're on the red carpet and I'm asked to stop for a photograph, I'll look around and Steve will have disappeared completely.

Playlist – the loved-up years:

New Order, 'World in Motion' – the song Steve was plugging, which got us talking. In fact, the first gift Steve gave me was a pair of huge, white baggy shorts with 'World in Motion' emblazoned down the side. I don't think I ever actually wore them, although my Dad did! When I hear this track it takes me back to our first summer of love, a hedonistic whirl of love, football, champagne and music. But it also seems to sum up my life – a moving kaleidoscope of motherhood, family, work, relationship; a set of disparate shards twisting together to make a beautiful, chaotic whole.

Cocteau Twins, 'Iceblink Luck' – Steve and I saw the Cocteau Twins play at the Town and Country Club, now The Forum, in Kentish Town, when we were first together. Everything about this heavenly love song sums up those heady early days.

The Rolling Stones, 'You Can't Always Get What You Want' – Steve wants the lyrics from this song on his gravestone. I'd never really listened to the Stones before I met Steve – they weren't a band Mum and Dad played. He made me listen carefully to the lyrics and I became hooked on the story and the drama of the track with its choir and crescendo.

Van Morrison, 'Angelou' – another musician I'd never heard. Steve and I spent hours sitting up late, drinking and listening to him during our first summer of love.

Steve and I were married in Great Brington, as I'd always known I would be. Frances was one of my bridesmaids. She was beautifully behaved, in a Frances sort of way. She hated having flowers in her hair – she hates anything remotely uncomfortable and is liable to suddenly whip her top off in public if it's bothering her. But I wanted all my girls to have flowers. My friend Jacqui Rees teaches children with learning disabilities and Frances just adores her – she was Frances's number one crush at the time. So Jacqui was given the onerous task of getting Frances to walk down the aisle without ripping the flowers out of her hair. The only way she could do it was to distract her by singing 'Only You' by The Flying Pickets, over and over. The whole time we were getting ready, Jacqui was singing the song in her deepest baritone, and each time she finished, Frances would bellow, full volume, 'Same again, Jacqui, same again.' Poor Jacqui sang that song the whole way up the aisle, whereupon Frances went and sat down on the floor next to the vicar and just in front of Steve and I – as though it was her whose blessing we were asking – rather than the vicar's. There she remained, with those flowers on her head, though slightly askew, throughout the service.

I loved our wedding day. We managed to make it quite unique and idiosyncratic and magical – and with that slight air of chaos which is the signature of any Whiley family event. We're incapable of doing calm and orderly. We had a country fair theme, with a magician going round the tables pulling rabbits out of hats and playing with fire, and stalls set up where you could play shove ha'penny and skittles and bowl, and wandering minstrels playing music. I remember heckling Steve a lot during the speech, which he also likes to say was the shape of things to come; but I found it impossible to just sit there passively while he did all the talking.

I never wanted the day to end. There's a photo of me on our wedding night, sitting in a chair, undressed but with my wedding dress lying over me, crying my eyes out, mascara all down my face, because I couldn't bear the fact that it was over.

From the surreal world of *Blue Radio*, I moved to Channel 4's *The Word* as a researcher in 1991 – Charlie Parsons, who'd been in charge of *Club X*, was the boss and he hired me. It was more or less the successor to *The Tube*, which had been presented by Paula Yates. *The Word* was presented by Terry Christian, a man with the most impossible job in TV, with Amanda de Cadenet providing light relief. It became a national institution, everybody's favourite post-pub programme. Looking back, I can see that this was my big break, although it didn't quite feel like that at the time. I became so music obsessed that I was given the job of booking bands to perform live. I made some very bad calls – I refused to allow Black Box to perform 'Ride on Time' on the show, and that song went on to be the biggest dance track of the early nineties. Fortunately I also made some good early calls. I booked Pulp and Blur and Primal Scream, and then when I discovered Grunge, Hole, Faith No More, and Rage Against the Machine. I scored a bit of a coup with the first ever UK TV performance of Nirvana. The show was famous for being risqué, but even its boundaries were stretched when lead singer Kurt Cobain announced that his new lover, Courtney Love, was 'The best fuck in the world'. There was always furious debate about the programme at Channel 4, but none of it was actually directed at me until I booked a Riot Grrrl band called Huggy Bear onto the show and one of them whacked poor Terry Christian, quite hard, on air. At work the following Monday, the producers were saying to me, 'What were you thinking of, booking Huggy Bear?' But by that Wednesday it had made the front cover of *Melody Maker*, and then all the producers started saying, 'Good work on Huggy Bear!' and my reputation was saved. Other great bands and great moments: The Manic Street Preachers, before Richey Edwards parked his car near the Severn Bridge and disappeared, rehearsing 'Love's Sweet Exile' all day, surprising us all by performing 'Repeat' with the lyrics 'Fuck Queen and Country' when the show went live; Dinosaur Jr playing on and on, refusing to stop, until the sound engineer was forced to silence them by literally pulling the plug. And then there was the resounding performance of 'Wild Thing' by an exceedingly inebriated Oliver Reed. We had a slot called 'I'd Do Anything To Be On TV', and I saw first-hand the lengths that the punters were prepared to go to, as members of the public would be filmed eating worms and bathing in maggots, kissing grannies and licking armpits.

Playlist – *The Word* years:

Nirvana, 'Smells Like Teen Spirit' – I've always said that I'd have been a moron not to have booked Nirvana on to *The Word*. But I'm eternally grateful that I'm not known in the industry as the person who turned Nirvana down; that I heard about them and realised their potential early on. I had some friends who were really into the grunge scene and had seen them in America and told me that I had to listen to them. 'Smells Like Teen Spirit' is four and a half minutes long and so we asked the band if they'd do a three-minute edit for the show. The answer came back: no. Charlie Parsons said that we'd have to tell them they couldn't come on but I argued their case – by then I was determined to have them. I'll never forget that day. Kurt Cobain was closeted in the dressing room, speaking to no one, Dave Grohl was like Tigger, bouncing around the studio, a bundle of irrepressible energy. For once, I decided not to be on duty and instead, shirking my responsibilities, I headed into the crowd and stood there in the audience at Kurt's feet. In the end, the show ran out of time and they ran credits over Nirvana and cut the end of the track. The band's entourage were furious and decided it was my fault – I was told to hide because they were out for my blood. I locked myself in an office upstairs until they'd finished rampaging around looking for me to kill and gone home.

L7, 'Pretend We're Dead' – it was such a rich time musically. I was watching this great girl band play when the lead singer suddenly turned to the camera and dropped her trousers, revealing to the world that she liked to go commando. The camera-man couldn't resist zooming in for a close up of her beaver. There was the usual response in the press, outrage but loads of coverage, and by then I'd been working there long enough to know that, ultimately, it was great TV. Maybe we got off lightly, because a couple of months later, at the Reading festival, the singer took out her tampon, live on stage, and hurled it into the crowd.

Faith No More, 'I Started a Joke' – another case of a band making the most of live TV and doing a totally different song to the one they had rehearsed. They were supposed to do The Commodores' 'Easy', but instead they threw water over Terry and did this cover of a Bee Gees track. Good though.

Rage Against the Machine, 'Killing in the Name' – I first saw them play at a tiny club in London, Subterranea. One of the best gigs I've ever been to, the band had so much energy and the audience were mad for it. I knew I had to get them on to *The Word* and I'm really proud that I did. They turned up wearing T-shirts emblazoned with FUCT and I remember having to delicately ask them if they'd allow us to cover it up with gaffer tape and being terrified that they'd storm off. They were very gracious about it, thankfully.

Primal Scream, 'Movin' On Up' – at the height of their hazy drug days, they were celebrating the success of their LP, *Screamadelica*, and had been given two slots on the show. Opening and closing. However, after their first performance they went AWOL – hitting the party trail, which meant that when they were needed to close the show they were nowhere to be seen . . . I resorted to looking on the TV monitors at the audience and trying to work out where the hell the band had gone with seconds before they played live. Hats off to Martin Duffy, the keyboard player who was incapable of standing, but managed to sit on a stool and play the song note-perfect.

Public Enemy, 'Shut 'Em Down' – I will never forget the time that Public Enemy – the world's most famous hip hop stars – were due to perform. I had left them in the dressing room but when I went to collect them for their live performance, they were nowhere to be seen. I ran into reception where Steve was sitting, and asked if he'd seen them. Bearing in mind there was Flavour Flav with his massive clock and Chuck D and the rest of P.E. were all wearing the biggest, brightest yellow puffa jackets I had ever seen – they were quite difficult to miss. Steve pointed out of the door towards McDonald's, 'they went thatta way.'

They had about six minutes to get themselves out of McDonald's, digest their burgers and get themselves into the studio and onto stage to perform, which is why I found myself standing in the middle of a busy Wembley street shouting at the world-famous Public Enemy and rounding up rap stars like sheep. And, take it from me, rap stars don't run – not even for live TV. They made it by the skin of their teeth, without breaking a sweat.

I was still working on *The Word* when, in the spring of 1993, I was asked to go in to Radio 1 and audition to do a week's cover for Mark Goodier. The idea was that a number of us would audition by doing a live show. It'd been years since I'd been behind a mike, but I was really keen to give it a go. I remember going down to the studio with Steve to rehearse. I had to borrow DLT's head-phones and, afterwards, I reeked of the notorious DLT aftershave, just couldn't get rid of the smell, it was so pungent. I wafted home. The rehearsals were a total disaster. It's something to do with the fact that I'm not an actor – I can't make-believe. I couldn't pretend that I was on air, live to the nation, because I wasn't. I remember seeing the look in the producer's eyes and my heart sinking to my boots.

Then, on the night, faced with the mike, alone in the studio and picturing that fictional audience of one out there, it all came together and I was fine – still sick with fear but fine. I did cock up on that first night, though. I remember looking at the mike and thinking, 'What next?' The Levellers sprang into my head for some reason and I started talking about them, quickly ran out of things to say, and found myself inventing a tour for them, and tour dates. God knows what I was doing. Perhaps I'd forgotten we weren't rehearsing. Then I got a furious call from the record company, saying, 'They're not touring!' They were utterly perplexed when I just replied, 'I know. Sorry about that.'

But it all came good. What Matthew Bannister, the new controller at Radio 1, suggested next was based on the feedback they'd had from the listeners: that Steve Lamacq and I do an evening show together for a short period, so they could see how things panned out.

I was amazed when I heard this – he and I are so different. Steve Lamacq had been an *NME* journalist and had a public profile, which I didn't have at all. And we were complete strangers. It was a bit like going on a blind date – live on air. We just bumbled through, chatting in between tracks and asking really obvious questions of one another.

Mark Goodier was really highly regarded back then, but he was Mr Pop, and I think the idea was to get him on to the daytime slot and have us replace him, doing something much more alternative in the evening, rather like Zane Lowe does now. After a trial period, we both got the call to go and see Matthew. It was one of those *Sliding Doors* moments – life-changing, a bit like me putting on that pair of headphones for the first time. I was thinking, 'Everything hinges on this moment.' Was he going to tell us to leave? That was happening all the time in those days of great change at Radio 1. But what he said was, 'I'd like you to be part of the new Radio 1,' and he offered us a permanent slot doing the *Evening Session*.

If you believe in fate, then it was fate that I ended up on radio. It was from this point – when I got involved with *Turn It Up* – that my life changed and I got happy. It was the launch pad for my career and, had I not endured three years of syntax and semantics, I might never have ended up working on radio.

The first days of being at Radio 1 were akin to the first few days at big school. Getting up in the morning knowing exactly what you're about to put on, because you've laid it all out the night before; crossing the threshold and walking into reception with a swagger borne out of an attempt at false confidence and trying to stop your knees from knocking with nerves. There were also the furtive glances over the shoulder to see when the Radio 1 security guards would suss you out as an impostor and challenge your right to be there:

'Excuse me, what do you think you're doing?'

'Um, I'm here to do the show – I'm one of the new DJs.'

'No chance. You don't look like a Radio 1 DJ. Get out of here. Now.'

Those conversations played out in my mind each and every day. In fact, on my return after having Coco, I was challenged several times by two zealous security officers questioning my assertion that I was at Radio 1 to do a show.

The reason I got the call to Radio 1 was that the producer of the *Evening Session*, which was then hosted by Mark Goodier, had seen me on the Power Station, was aware that I'd booked Nirvana on *The Word*, and thought I was worth a punt. His name is Jeff Smith and he's now Head of Music at Radio 2. I pretty much owe him my career. He was a fastidious producer and a harsh critic – not in a nasty way – he was more a man of frowns and disappointed sighs, which were far more crushing. When Jeff gave you a compliment, you were like a dog thrown a morsel of food. I tried out on my own, as did Steve Lamacq, Claire Sturgess and Richard Easter.

Jeff obviously spotted our strengths and weaknesses, and decided that our two halves would make a whole presenter, and put us together on air in a matter of weeks. I remember we did one pilot in which I was disastrous – I'm incapable of going through the motions and can only ever pull it off when I know I'm live on air – thriving on energy and adrenaline. Steve and I barely knew each other, just knew of each other – he was an *NME* journalist with a fierce passion for music and was clever with words. Initially we were wary of and polite to one another, 'Would you like to come out of this record, or shall I?'

'After you.'

'My pleasure.'

But by the end of the first week – and nightly trips to the Yorkshire Grey – it was a doddle, and we slipped into a rhythm easily. The things that bonded us were a love of cider and DMs, both big passions of ours. I'm grateful to Steve for many things – he was always faintly protective of me – he introduced me to greyhound racing, peanuts and the Good Mixer. And boy, could we whinge! We put the music industry to rights night after night – the independent bands and labels vs the big corporate labels, why this band were shite, that band were going to change the face of music . . .

Steve was also my fashion advisor once we started being photographed and having to go out on stage. 'Hair up or hair down?' was the most common question. Our roles on the show became quite defined in the end. Steve was the musical purist and hated the more trivial features we did – one memorable feature was the thirty-minute menu where bands would come in and talk us through a recipe, Coolio did a chicken curry and Jarvis turned up with his ingredients in a plastic bag – Steve thought this detracted from the music, whereas I quite enjoyed the feature, and that led quite naturally to our separation. He continued to champion new bands and debate issues while I went over to the dark side: the mainstream.

Looking back, there were comical moments when musical differences led to door slamming and walls were punched in temper, but Steve and I rarely had stand-up confrontations. Nope, we were magnificently moody instead. Pity the poor producer who sat in the studio when we were both in a major sulk with each other. The music might have been blaring out at eleven decibels, but in the studios, there'd be silence. Just two mute presenters who didn't utter a word to each other save for on-air jovial banter. But these were rare occurrences, and I'm sure other double acts had their off days too. Who knows what tense words were said between Canon and Ball once the show was over? But, slowly our friendship blossomed. The fact that we had such different musical tastes began to work really well, because it broadened our playlists hugely, and there was a natural way for us to split our links – Therapy? or Kingmaker, Steve; Björk or Portishead, me. It meant that my Steve was left holding the baby each night, but we still managed to be together often as a little family unit of three.

The whole Britpop phenomenon was exploding just as we started on the *Evening Session*, and it became something of a gift to the station; certainly no other stations were playing these great bands right at the beginning. When the Oasis single, 'Columbia', came out, we played it on the *Evening Session*. But it wasn't until we got Oasis to come in, months before they had a hit, that we got a taste of that Gallagher magic, and could see they were going to be huge. We booked them on to *Sound City*, the precursor to the Radio 1 *Big Weekend*, which was the first live radio event they'd ever done. I decided that I'd nail my flag to the Oasis mast, while Steve Lamacq remained firmly in the Blur camp – he had known the band for a while. My only connection with Blur was that, back in the days of *WPFM*, I'd interviewed them and they'd made me cry, they were such tricky characters, so I was happy for Steve Lamacq to 'have' them. Even now, I get the fear interviewing Blur, I think they'd probably still make me cry. Damon Albarn has such a wicked way about him; the second the fader goes up, he adopts a persona quite apart from his normal, affable self. You'll ask him how he is and he'll react as though you've just said something incredibly critical about his last album.

I went up to Newcastle to see an Oasis gig, travelling with the band. They'd played one song when someone in the audience threw a bottle and it hit Liam in the face, hard, and cut him above the eye. Liam was bleeding and furious – it was when they were still very young and very angry. 'That's it, we're quitting,' Liam shouted. Both brothers were hurling abuse randomly. They came off stage and refused to go back on, and the gig descended into a near riot; we all had to be bundled out the back and driven away, fast, to avoid the crowd. We ended up back at the hotel with Noel and Liam so angry and so fired up; it really was quite horrible to see. I spent hours that night trying to be the peacemaker between the brothers and calm everything down. I've always been fascinated by their relationship. In the beginning it seemed that Noel was the quiet one and that Liam was very much the boss of the band, but I think that's far from the truth. Noel is the older brother, completely in charge, and calling the shots, and Liam is the one looking for approval. Both are very funny men. Noel has a razor-sharp wit and Liam who talks in riddles that might just be unfathomably deep. (One of my prize possessions is a recording called 'Wibbling Rivalry' of Liam and Noel Gallagher being interviewed by *NME* journo John Harris in Glasgow, 1994, and getting into an unbelievably foul-mouthed argument. It's really very funny – and worth looking up. The transcript is on the internet.)

I remember the Manics coming in just after Richey Edwards had disappeared. Nicky Wire and I talked about what he thought might've happened to Richey, where he might be, and he came very close to breaking down. I could see that the interview was incredibly painful for him, but at the same time cathartic. The *Evening Session* was like a school play with an assortment of key characters: Oasis and Blur I've mentioned, but The Manics were also firm favourites. Other regulars were Justine Frischmann (Elastica), supercool first lady of Britpop, Louise Wener (Sleeper) – the indie boy's wet dream was the savvy second lady and lyricist and also Martin Rossiter (Gene) – sweet man, beautiful songs.

Playlist – the *Evening Session* years:

Oasis, 'Columbia' – if I close my eyes, I can remember so clearly the moment when our producer came in and handed us a piece of vinyl and said, 'This has come from Alan McGee, you've got to listen to it.' Alan McGee was such a force that, if he was putting himself behind a band, you knew you had to sit up and take notice. We put on the record and knew that we were listening to something special. I remember having an even stronger reaction a few years later, when I played their second album, *(What's the Story) Morning Glory?*. I walked out of the kitchen to do something and then stopped, arrested by the opening bars of 'Don't Look Back in Anger'. I'll never forget the chills down my spine as I listened to that song for the first time. I've always been a fan of the soft underbelly of Oasis – the songs Noel sings have a sweetness to them which contrasts so strongly to the swagger of Liam's.

'Masterplan', 'Slide Away', 'Half the World Away', all classics.

Blur, 'Parklife' – Blur were very much Steve Lamacq's territory, as I've said. They had a relationship before the *Evening Session* and I didn't feel it was my place to intrude. I remember Steve coming in and telling me how important the album was, that it was going to be the work of their career. He was right, and this track and its iconic video launched them into the stratosphere in a way they couldn't have forseen, until tensions within the band brought about their demise. And this year we get to see Blur once more, reformed and headlining at Glastonbury.

Boo Radleys, 'Wake Up Boo!' – This song reminds me of the time when we were playing all these Britpop bands on the *Evening Session*. We played the Boo Radleys, then the band came up with this amazing pop track, and suddenly they were getting played on *The Breakfast Show*. Chris Evans was partly responsible for the crossover, of course – he was incredibly generous in championing what Steve Lamacq and I were doing in the evenings.

Green Day, 'Basketcase' – a superbly angry track, which suited Steve Lamacq and my mood during those years. This was the track that we played when we felt as though it was us against the world. The lyrics are self-pitying and magnificent, and I kind of think of it as our anthem.

When I joined the station, the first stirrings of Matthew Bannister's Radio 1 revolution were taking place – that's how I came to be there, after all. Johnny Beerling had been controller for twenty-five years, and when he was succeeded by Matthew Bannister, it marked the end of an era. But the change didn't happen overnight, and when I arrived, the legendary DJs were all still there – Simon Bates, DLT, Johnny Walker, Bruno Brookes, Fluff Freeman. In the first weeks Simon Bates sailed by me, time and again, oblivious – I might've been the cleaner. I'd come in on the weekend sometimes to practise and once Fluff Freeman was there in the next studio doing his show and he called out, 'All right, Jo?' I was amazed – he knew who I was! There was a very obvious divide back then, between the 'personality' DJs and the very few for whom it was all about music. John Peel was obviously in the latter camp. He and Johnnie Walker sat on the third floor; the likes of DLT sat on the fourth floor. Each DJ had their own little fiefdom; it was very much them and their producer against the rest of the world.

The only other female DJ was Annie Nightingale, who'd been there since 1970, and is still going strong today. She's survived because she is so great – she's definitely a DJ who cares about the music rather than celebrity (such as it is) and she very much kept to herself, behind those ever-present sunglasses. It was years before I even knew that Annie had children. She chose to protect herself by keeping her family under wraps. Annie was someone I listened to as a fan on the Sunday night request show, guessing when she'd say her famous 'hi'. I loved the music she played and enjoyed the relationship she had with her listeners. As a DJ, if there is anyone I aspired to be, it was Annie. Since I began at Radio 1, she has been nothing less than fabulous – encouraging in every way and protective when the going got tough for me.

With the arrival of Matthew, there were these distant rumblings among the titans, like a volcano, and I think a number of the old guard – DLT, Steve Wright and Simon Bates – sensed that their time was up. Hysteria was in the air – everyone was feeling deeply paranoid. I knew DLT's producer quite well and she described how he'd turned up one morning and said to her, 'You're not going to like what happens on the show today,' and she was frozen, wondering what he was going to do. And then he read out a long statement about how he didn't like what was happening on Radio 1 and so it was time for him to go. I admired it in a way – it meant he had control over his departure – but it caused an absolute furore. And then the ratings began to fall, as all the big names from the nation's favourite radio station, the people to whom the public had tuned into for years, began to leave.

One of the big changes that Matthew Bannister oversaw was the creation of playlists for the DJs. I was in the studio one day and Johnnie Walker was next door to me and he buzzed through and said, 'If this is the future of Radio 1 then I can't be a part of it.' He couldn't accept the loss of control – he was no longer allowed to choose exactly what he played, seconds before he played it. Johnny is someone I have so much respect for, he's a maverick and a serious broadcaster and so he headed off to Radio 2 and he's had a great career there since.

I know how lucky I was to be there at the beginning of the new Radio 1 and to have had Matthew's support. He was always incredibly kind and encouraging – we were very much Bannister's children, and gradually Steve Lamacq and I worked out our rhythm on the show. The weird aspect of a specialist show is that you're basically telling the world what they should be listening to. Back when I started with Steve there was still a sense of having to stuff songs you liked into a 'genre'. There was britpop and there'd been grunge. It was a bit of a hangover from the days of the power of *NME*, I think. Everything had to be pigeon-holed.

Radio 1 DJs are required to do quite a bit of extra-curricular work, something I hadn't quite faced up to when I started. Thankfully, Matthew Bannister did away with the roadshows as they had been – Smiley Miley, Bits 'n' Pieces etc. and DJs playing the top twenty to a group of people in a desolate seaside town. (John Peel was always hilarious on the subject of his loathing of the roadshow and did his best to subvert them and send them up.) The road shows have since evolved into Radio 1's Big Weekend and the first step in this evolution was Sound City, which Steve Lamacq and I became involved in once we took over the *Evening Session*. We'd be desperate to book our favourite new bands to play, but the producers would be telling us we had to also make the show accessible to the daytime listeners, who might then tune in to the *Evening Session*. We'd fight like cats and dogs over who was going to introduce a band like Oui-3, that we felt would damage our indie credentials – M-People was our nadir for quite a while. I have nothing against M-People person-ally, but they weren't exactly what our show was supposed to represent. We'd be on the side of the stage, squabbling over who'd introduce them. I always seemed to lose the battle, and I'd find myself trudging out there. I do remember Steve once going on and saying, 'Ladies and Gentlemen, give it up for Oui-3!' and then racing back to the side of the stage, dropping to his knees, head in hands, rocking backwards and forwards groaning, 'I don't know what came over me. I never say "Give it up"!' After that, it became a running joke between us. The more we loathed a band, the louder we'd shout 'Give it up!'

Looking back now, I realise what a strange time it was to be at Radio 1. I was finally doing what I'd always wanted to do, brim-ming with excitement and enthusiasm, and all the while the big names were leaving the station and the ratings were plum-meting, falling through the floor. People were switching off in their millions. The *Sun* regarded the purge of all the big DJs as an outrage and ran the headline 'Sliding Down the Bannister'. It became a front-page campaign, the sliding bannister, which ran daily details of the latest fall in figures. It was felt that Matthew was trendifying – Londonifying – Radio 1 rather than listening to the people, the workers up and down the country who were their true audience. This was nonsense, of course. Matthew did what needed to be done and he really hit the ground running. I think he must've felt that he had to act quickly, or not at all. A more cowardly person might've baulked as the ratings fell and tried to get some of those big names back onboard, but Matthew just ploughed on regardless. With the explosion of the internet and music TV, Radio 1 had to become commercial and move with the times or it wouldn't have survived. This is a challenge it still faces and has successfully adapted to, with its phenomenal online presence, driven by Andy Parfitt.

I was incredibly green when I started at Radio 1. I'd barely even left the country. As a child, my only trip 'overseas' was to Guernsey, something that's become a bit of a family joke – I remember Steve roaring with laughter when I told him proudly about our first holiday 'abroad'. There were a couple of trips further afield in my late teens, to France and to Greece, and our honeymoon in St Lucia, but I'd probably been on a plane less than half a dozen times. Shortly after Steve Lamacq and I started doing the *Evening Session*, I was sent to Las Vegas to do a special programme with the band James. India was still little and I'd never been away from her and Steve before. I was excited about going and thought I'd be fine about leaving my family, until I got on the plane. I hadn't even registered how long it would take to fly to LA – I was that naïve. As we were taking off, the pilot announced that the flight was eleven-plus hours long. I had what I realise now was a panic attack – I remember sitting there, shaking and sweating. I'd just managed to relax a little when there was an enormous crash, like a thunderclap, and I felt the plane drop, making my stomach fall out through the floor beneath my feet. In those few seconds I knew with absolute clarity that I was going to die. Then the pilot came on and congratulated us: we'd been struck by lightning – a very rare occurrence, apparently. I didn't exactly feel privileged, I felt petrified. Worse was to come. We landed in LA and got onto a tiny plane to fly to Vegas and the storm seemed to follow us. The hostesses stayed strapped into their seats for the entire short flight, rain lashed the windows, the plane swooped up and down and I was utterly beside myself with fear. To make matters worse, I was with someone from James's record company who I barely knew, and I didn't feel able to throw myself sobbing in her lap, which is what I desperately wanted to do. It couldn't have been a worse beginning to what has been a lifetime of travelling for work. We arrived in Vegas in one piece and found we were booked to stay in a motel straight out of a horror film, complete with roaches the size of small dogs, filthy net curtains and a flashing red neon sign with half the letters missing. I remember calling Steve and wailing down the phone. But then Marsha, the girl from the record company, decided to take control of the situation and marched us both to better accommodation – a wonderfully cheesy themed hotel, shaped like a pirate ship. Things were on the up from there on. We watched James play the next night and they dedicated 'Sit Down' to us and tweaked the lyrics to make light of our turbulent plane ride.

I think Matthew and Andy turned things around for Radio 1 when they hired Chris Evans to do *The Breakfast Show*. It was the moment when the press began to run with the idea that exciting things were afoot at the station, rather than that it was in a state of terminal decline. Chris was something else, of course. These days he's calm and sweet and as nice as pie. Back then, he was just a ball of manic energy and, as I remembered from the Power Station, he had a nasty habit of exposing himself, all the time. You'd pass him in the corridor and whoops, there it'd be, out on display. After a while, we all stopped seeing it. Chris was an incredibly supportive colleague though, he understood that the station was the sum of its parts and had to gel as a whole in order to survive, which was so completely different from the bunker mentality of the old guard. He did Steve Lamacq and me a huge favour by talking up the *Evening Session* on *The Breakfast Show* and that had an enormous effect on our ratings – a lot of people started to tune in. He brought it together for all of us at Radio 1, and I'll always be grateful to him. It was very difficult for all of us when things started to go wrong for Chris – there were internal rumblings, the paparazzi stories, the eighteen-hour drinking binges with his eighteen-year-old wife. I think in the end he burned out, something that I've seen time and again with hard-living breakfast jocks. But I was really sorry when he left. It was a real loss, personally, and to the station.

These days, of course, Chris is the king of *Drive Time* at Radio 2 and doing incredibly well. He and I met the Queen together a few years back, which was a surreal occasion. God knows what the Chris of old would have done, but he was charm itself. I have a picture of the two of us with her, laughing our heads off. People have asked me countless times what we talked about and, if they've seen the picture, what was so funny? I always answer truthfully and say that I have no idea – I really can't remember. All I know is that I was beside myself with anxiety and was convinced I'd fall over trying to curtsey or that I'd develop Tourettes Syndrome and say fuck. Neither thing happened, and I remember that she was very careful to put us at ease with a joke and that she confessed to not listening to either of our shows. It was like meeting someone from another planet, though. We were probably laughing with relief at not having messed up.

I made my first foray into the world of television during those early years at Radio 1. I'd done a little bit of presenting on *Indie Chart* at the Power Station and I'd worked on *The Word*, so I knew all about putting a TV programme together, but I was comfortable being hidden away behind the mike. Then Steve Lamacq and I were approached to present *Top of the Pops*. It was part of the general mood of change – they were mixing everything up a little to see what worked. It was terrifying – *TOTP* is such an institution. I'd watched Jimmy Savile and DLT presenting old editions of *UK Gold*, and to think that now I was doing that too, and that it was just possible that people might still be watching me do it in twenty years' time, was very strange.

Let's be honest, we're not TV people, either of us: Steve Lamacq and I have great faces for radio and a radio mindset. This was national television, too, and we'd be there with all the bands waiting to play and producers yelling in our ears and it was live, mostly, so you'd know you had eleven seconds to do your link and if you took longer the whole programme would be ruined. And we had to introduce some acts that represented the opposite of what we were doing on the *Evening Session*. I remember wracking my brains to come up with something to say about the Spice Girls, other than 'Give it up . . .' But I also remember great moments – Garbage playing, for example, just such a great band with an amazing frontwoman in Shirley Manson. When bands like Garbage were on, there was no need to 'Give it up'. Then I was asked to present *TOTP* solo, alternating with Zoe Ball and Jayne Middlemiss, and between us we presented most of the shows in 1997. I really missed working with Steve Lamacq. The three of us 'nineties girls' (as they dubbed us) did the *TOTP* Christmas Special together which I found excruciating. Zoe's tall, she's also very slim and fabulous-looking, and Jayne has a Page Three figure and I remember lining up with them for a photo shoot in my DMs and a dress I'd found at Camden Market (this was the pre-stylist era). I know that other presenters have managed to imbue their style (or lack of it) with just a whiff of irony, but I've never succeeded, to me I just appeared awkward.

Steve Lamacq and I presented the *Evening Session* from September 1993 to the beginning of 1997. They were great years. There was a Radio 1 ad out at the time in which various people from the station, DJs, producers, etc., were photographed in the studios with a bit of personal information about themselves. Mine was 'Grew up at Miss Selfridge and down the bottom of the playing field at school'. In actual fact, I think that I did most of my real growing up on air at Radio 1. (Tied in with that ad campaign were vast billboards throughout the country, including a shot of me in the studio. One appeared in Northampton, much to the delight of my family, who dragged me down there to have a photo taken beneath it. Frances was beside herself with pleasure every time she drove past, and was then grief-stricken when I began to look a little tatty and was eventually taken down.)

In 1997, India started school. Up until then, my night job had been fine, because I'd be with her in the day before going to the studio in the evening and leaving her with Steve. But once she started school she began to really struggle with me heading out the door at bedtime. We'd both been emotional wrecks as she was peeled from my arms and the door closed behind me. I'd been doing a bit of covering for Lisa I'Anson's lunchtime programme, which I'd loved – there's no pressure involved in filling in for someone else's show; it was like being given a great toy to play with and I had a laugh, and enjoyed introducing tracks I'd been playing in the evenings to a daytime crowd. Then Lisa had a bit of an episode and left Radio 1, having failed to turn up to present her show from Ibiza. Andy Parfitt, who was Matthew's number two, took me for a cup of tea at the Heights, which was Radio 1's HQ back then, legendary and very much the world of the old school, fusty but with amazing views over London. I'd only ever been up there for Johnnie Walker's leaving do. Andy asked me where I wanted to go; did I have a grand plan, would I consider a daytime slot? I'd never thought too hard about the future, so it seemed simplest to be positive. So I said, 'I'm up for doing pretty much anything you might offer me, I'm sure it'd be absolutely fine.' And that was that – shortly afterwards I was offered Lisa's slot. I knew it'd mean leaving the still relatively free world of night-time radio and moving to one more dominated by ratings and pre-programmed playlists, but I had India and my Steve to think about. So I said yes, but on one condition: that I had four 'free plays' per session or one every half an hour – four tracks that were entirely my choice. I was amazed when they said yes, but it's been great; I've held on to it. It's become something of a calling card for me.

Leaving the *Evening Session* meant saying goodbye to Steve Lamacq, which was a real wrench. He has a reputation for being quite dour, but he's a real softie, a genuinely kind-hearted man and he's remained a great friend. And, once I'd got used to being alone, I felt freer. It was time for me to try out things for myself and to relax into doing my own thing, without agonising over whether Steve was going to hate what I wanted to play. It was a pretty short slot, an hour and three quarters, and didn't feel too daunting. It was to be called the *Lunchtime Social* – a nod to that legendary nineties Sunday club bash, the *Heavenly Social*. So I flew solo for the first time and I adored it. I could be enthusiastic about stuff I loved and as I got good ratings, my confidence grew.

I was never going to be a personality DJ – a Chris Moyles or Chris Evans – ideally suited to breakfast because it's more about them chatting to the world than the music they're playing. There's a thing on the radio called a 'programme clock', which is basically the number of tracks programmed to be played per hour. Moyles has the lowest number of tracks per hour at the station because he's a talker. I'm not a talker; I want to play music. But this change meant I could go to work while my daughter was at school and be a mother to her when she was home. And see my husband, too.

When I started, it was the last days of DJs and their producers deciding what they'd play, which is a world apart from what happens now, with playlists and playlist committees. It's a dark art, involving producers, audience research and passionate DJs. In some ways you can say that it's more egalitarian – we're playing what the people want to hear, even if it's not always what

I want to hear. This is often a revelation to the listener, who some-times assumes that if you play it, you like it. I've had to learn to resist the temptation to announce live on air that I absolutely loathe a particular track. What I learned to focus on was a sense of balance; if I had to play one track I hated, there'd be far more that I loved.

But even daytime radio was much freer back then. My producer was Ben Cooper, who's now the deputy head of Radio 1. (Later on he was Chris Moyles's producer, and he dealt with Moyles's tendency to get overexcited by having a buzzer he pressed whenever he thought Chris had overstepped the mark. God know how often he's had to push that thing.) When I look back, I laugh about how we ran things, it was all so basic. We didn't do live music or many interviews; it was just me and the tracks. Partly this had to do with the massive overhaul taking place at Radio 1. The old guard might've felt that they'd had their wings clipped, but there was so much going on, so many DJs starting out or going to new slots, and there wasn't a coordinated team of producers controlling what was happening. The era of DLT playing snooker live on air, complete with the sound of the balls smashing together and dropping into the pockets, was well and truly over. But for a while it was replaced with relative anarchy. A man who became a legend in his own lunchtime, Trevor Dann, and Matthew Bannister, Head of Entertainment, began making the rules. We were told that there were to be no hooks, no games, no features, no competitions. All that went out the window. When I did start doing interviews, I was told that they were to be no longer than three minutes. Over the years that's all changed, and today my show has all of these things and more, because the listeners love all the bells and whistles. Sometimes my interviews run throughout an entire session, interspersed with tracks. But I can understand what Matthew and Trevor were trying to do back then. It was crucial to cut away everything from the past and start afresh. (They didn't get every-thing right – it was about this time that Trevor announced that

Radio 1 would never play Radiohead. I think the Beatles and Status Quo were also casualties of Trevor's musical censorship.)

John Peel once helped me out with the White Stripes. It was when I'd just moved from the *Evening Session* to having a daytime show, and I was anxious about 'selling out' – moving to a programme with playlists and far more commercial music. The White Stripes were in the studio and they were giving me a slightly hard time and, while a track was on, I cut back to them and heard Jack White saying something about the fact that I was playing Kylie Minogue and what the hell was he doing on this show? It wasn't particularly unreasonable of him to ask the question or even very surprising, and these days if I hear something like that, it's like water off a duck's back. But, back then, it really hit home because he voiced all of my anxieties in that single, scathing remark. I must've gone wailing to John about it, because I remember him being extraordinarily eloquent in his outrage on my behalf. He reminded me why I'd gone to the daytime slot and said that bands should remember that they needed Radio 1 as much as we needed them. As far as John was concerned, it was great that I was there in the daytime and still really keen to introduce the world to new talent. In any case, I think John must've 'had a word' because the next time we met, Jack was charm personified, and has been that way ever since.

I had two similar experiences with bands coming on to the show and making it clear they didn't want to be there, back when I was first doing daytime radio. When Radiohead came on to do my show, I'd been assured by the record company that they were keen to come on, but they made it abundantly clear that they weren't and the result was a pretty disastrous interview. Green Day turned up and refused to come into the studio, saying that they wanted to see a list of the questions I was planning to ask first. I said that I couldn't provide a list – that's not how I conduct interviews, I would just be chatting to them. A stand-off ensued and then, while I was on air, they suddenly all piled into the studio and started behaving like naughty schoolboys, very shouty and out of control. I think those were my two worst on-air moments and my reaction to them had a lot do with my own anxiety about whether I'd 'sold out' by moving to daytime radio. In both cases I think the real culprit was the record company forcing their acts into something, while at the time assuring me that they were keen to do it.

In 1997, Channel 4's Jo Wallace approached me with the idea of doing my own late-night TV programme, *The Jo Whiley Show* produced by two ex-*Word* mavericks, Martin Cunning and Chris Fouracre. The idea was to have three celebrities discussing recent tracks and gossiping about acts, pieced together with new music videos and a live performance. They'd choose very different people who were likely to have opposing views and musical tastes, in the hope of creating controversy. I found it incredibly stressful because it plunged me firmly into the limelight. I suddenly had to think seriously about my appearance. Footwear was a nightmare. I wouldn't have that problem now: I have latterly developed a shoe fetish worthy of Imelda Marcos; but back then I felt that I could just about work out what to wear, but I could not for the life of me think beyond DMs, which the producers made clear were a big no-no. So I wound up barefoot more often than not. I was stunned by the level of vitriol aimed at my physical appearance – it's amazing what is considered fair comment by some in the press. I was doing really well in my career, and had just been named DJ of the Year at the Sony Music Awards, and yet it was considered OK to devote column inches to how I was better suited to radio and how badly I dressed.

The other thing that made doing the show very stressful was that its aim was to be controversial, which isn't necessarily in my nature. I'd have the producers yelling in my ear, telling me to ask difficult questions, putting words that didn't feel like mine into my mouth, and I managed to really upset a few people. One was Robbie Williams, who till then I'd been on really good terms with. Neil Hannon from The Divine Comedy was on the show. The Divine Comedy was about to tour with Robbie, and somehow the talk turned to him. Neil was faintly mocking – but then he's faintly mocking of everything and everyone. Robbie was probably at home, watching, and feeling low because his beloved grandmother had just died, and he felt that none of us were being sufficiently kind or supportive. He felt that I, in particular, should've weighed in on his behalf. But that wasn't what I was supposed to be doing – I was supposed to be stirring up trouble. Robbie let it be known that he was furious. Shortly afterwards, he played at a Radio 1 *Big Weekend*. I was backstage, and was told by some of his people to stay away from him. But I thought I could patch things up if I went and apologised. I really couldn't believe he could be that angry about it. I went and found him, and to say he was angry was an understatement. Robbie was going out with Nicole Appleton then, and I had to make my way through the sisters and their entourage who all looked on shocked while he lambasted me. He let me have it, full force. He was shouting, just incandescent. There was nothing I could say to calm him down. I came away really shaken. He went on stage thirty minutes later, and I was terrified that he'd say something on stage, because I knew India was out in the audience on Steve's shoulders, loving Robbie. Afterwards I felt that maybe he was right – I wished I'd stuck my neck out and defended him. If it'd been the show I'd wanted it to be, it would've been about coaxing secrets and stories from people by encouraging them to confide in me. But then we probably would have had fewer viewers, as I doubt that was what the public were after. I think that now we live in more generous times; people are more open and respectful of different kinds of music. Back then it was cool to be a cynic. One repeated criticism levelled at me was that I was no Jeremy Paxman and they were right – I'd far rather be a friend than an enemy.

Two years went by before I saw Robbie again, when he came in to be interviewed by Simon Mayo. We chatted and he made it clear that I'd been forgiven, but there's a coolness between us now, which I regret to this day.

But I have some fantastic memories from doing *The Jo Whiley Show*: Lenny Kravitz and Ultra Naté, from Brooklyn Heights and Baltimore respectively, looking slightly bemused as Malcolm MacLaren described his 'discovery' of Afrika Bambaataa and the whole hip-hop phenomenon; Huey from Fun Lovin' Criminals, so 'relaxed' that he was horizontal in his chair, outlining what he planned to do to the youngest member of Hanson, after the ten year old had ticked him off for smoking a spliff backstage at a concert; Goldie, on the subject of George Michael's unfortunate encounter with a police officer in a public loo in LA, asking why the man, given his fame and money, couldn't just have had a wank at home; Jason Donovan in a state of high chemical confusion, being terribly affable and sweet, but making no sense at all, and towards the end of the show turning to Neil Tennant from Pet Shop Boys and asking, with a look of wide-eyed innocence, 'Are you gay?'

I hadn't been doing the *Lunchtime Social* for very long when Diana, Princess of Wales died. As I've described earlier, my sister Frances made her unique tribute to the passing of the People's Princess. It was such a strange time to be on air. Radio 1 has a contingency plan for emergencies; there's a little cupboard with CDs in it with three different ranges of music. CD 1 is all instrumental, CD 2 sombre vocal tracks, CD 3 is aimed at getting people to get over their grief and cheer up. None of these seemed quite appropriate somehow, we were just feeling our way because none of us had experienced anything quite like the national outpouring of grief. It seemed best to say very little; Matthew Bannister judged this perfectly, I think. People were fed up with the rolling news and some of the other stations did too much talking and anecdotal stuff about how particular DJs had known her personally – 'Diana was always a personal friend of Capital Radio,' that sort of thing. There were a few faux pas, and I have to confess to having been on air when one of them was made – although it was a playlist song, not my own choice. We played The Smiths track, 'There is a Light That Never Goes Out', which refers to a bus crash and has the famous lyric about ways to die. That was, ahem, most unfortunate. It was like being in a state of suspended animation, and it went on and on, day after day. We were all waiting for the mood to lift, but for the longest time it didn't, and so I'd go in and spend another day saying as little as possible and endlessly playing the P. Diddy song written for Notorious B.I.G., 'I'll be Missing You'.

When John Peel died, the country seemed to go into deep mourning again, and I remember feeling the pressure of gauging our listeners' mood and working out what they wanted. I was grieving myself and it was so hard to know what to say about him and to find the words to express what his loss meant to me personally, to everyone at Radio 1 and to his listeners. The best way to do this was through music which, after his family, was the love of John's life. I lost count of the number of times we played 'Teenage Kicks'. Again, it was quite a while before things seemed to return to normal.

The big change is the number of women DJs (and producers) at the station. As I've said, when I started, there was just Annie Nightingale, Janice Long and me DJing, and relatively few women producers, but a whole floor of secretaries in a typing pool. The programming was based on the premise that the DJs would be men. Annie Nightingale has spoken with feeling about the horror of being expected to judge wet T-shirt competitions. I still shudder when I recall broadcasting from Magaluf in Mallorca, from the BCM nightclub, home of the half-naked lager-drinking Brit on tour. I was with Scott Mills, with whom I share a close bond based around our mutual horror of public appearances. I had to get up on stage and run a probe up and down a bikini-clad girl's body to detect whether she'd had sex the night before, which is possibly the worst thing I've ever done on air.

Somehow Scott convinced me that I should do it. I'm such a soft touch. He still owes me one for that.

I hadn't been at Radio 1 for long before other women began joining the station. The nineties were very much the era of the ladette and *Loaded*. Thankfully, that moment seems to have passed, and there doesn't seem to be such an emphasis on women having to 'be' something – sexy, tomboys, or whatever. Zoe Ball was the ultimate ladette in the eyes of the tabloids; she was brought in as a personality DJ and, for a while, she was riding high, partying hard, talking about the antics of the night before on her breakfast show, getting endless coverage and being followed everywhere by paparazzi. Zoe and I go back a long way; we worked together as researchers on *The Word*, long before she became famous and I joined Radio 1, and we've always been friends. We were invited to their wedding at Babington House, which was wonderful. India, in typical style, managed to blag her way into the wedding party. The bridesmaid and page boy, who were Norman's niece and nephew, were playing flutes as part of the ceremony. India got hold of a recorder from somewhere and, before we knew it, she'd marched up there and was standing with the two mini-flautists, tootling away and looking angelic, if a little scruffy.

I think that Simon Mayo felt that he didn't have his Radio 1 contract renewed because of his age. He had done breakfast for a long time and then followed that with the mid-morning slot, 10 a.m. to 1.45 p.m. I'm older now than he was when he left. But he was such an intelligent man, rather sophisticated, and the show reflected that. It was bittersweet, taking over from him, because I was really excited to be getting the job, but I liked and admired Simon so much. The last time he broadcast the show he made a great farewell speech, saying he wasn't going to do a DLT because he had nothing to complain about and, in any case, he was still being employed by the BBC so burning his bridges would be a little short-sighted.

At first, being on air for nearly four hours seemed exhausting. But by then I'd discovered how much I like interviewing people, which hadn't happened often on the *Lunchtime Social* because there wasn't time. Now I had the freedom to get people in to talk. We started out just getting bands in, but gradually we broadened it out to include other people in the public eye, primarily actors. I think that this partly reflects the way the world has changed. There's a sort of elite club of the very famous, and everyone seems to know who is and isn't a member. Once you're a member, then the world is fascinated by you, regardless of whether you're Bono or Bear Grylls, Nigella Lawson or Victoria Beckham. I don't want to disappoint, but all of those people are just like you and me. They're just as paranoid about their weight and what they eat, whether their bum looks big in their jeans, and whether their hairline is receding. And as an interviewer, it's these human frailties that you want to tap into.

Sometimes the interviews are a nightmare, of course, but others go brilliantly. I try not to get hung up about what is said about me as a public figure, whether it's to do with my appearance or my work – you have to just let that sort of thing glide over you or you'd go crazy. There is one thing I hate, though, and it hits the spot every time I come across it, and that's the suggestion that I'm being fake when I'm talking to people. I try really hard to be myself, no matter who I have in front of me, and in fact I think that I'm pretty much incapable of being anyone but myself. There are those who I know immediately are going to be a joy to work with – Noel Gallagher springs to mind (although Oasis went through that classic fame cycle: a joy to be with when they were first on the *Evening Session*, then difficult and beyond cool, then rueful and wise once they'd got used to stellar life and calmed down a little). I try to make an 'ordinary' connection. It's always great if they've got children – there's a bond then, and with a brood the size of mine, I generally have a child that's roughly the same age as the person I'm talking to. I clicked with Adele in spite of the fact that she's not much older than India because she's so charming and down-to-earth. We laughed a lot about her school days, and she told me all about her obsession with the Spice Girls and how she wanted to be Ginger Spice. I try to scratch beneath the surface a little, rather than coming at my subject from a showbiz angle.

Some interviews run such a pre-programmed course that everyone involved, interviewer and interviewee, just switch to autopilot – there are standard questions, standard answers. When's the new album out? What's the material like? Are you going to be touring? Are you excited about this new film? Some artists want that, in fact, won't let you past it. But if the encounter is going to be meaningful to the listeners, we have to offer them more. I've done formulaic interviews like that and ended up feeling as though I've just had a one-night stand – we've both acted as though we were having the time of our lives, but really we were faking it, and you come away feeling a bit deflated.

You have to keep it all in perspective, of course – why should Britney Spears open up to me? These people go through the publicity mill countless times each year. I had Kelly Clarkson on the show recently, and I asked her about getting her fans to film themselves lip-syncing to her latest single. She paused for a minute and then said, 'I was going to just go along with this, but I can't lie. I have NO recollection of doing that. Did I really?' I just wanted to hug her. It was a world away from the glazed expression and polite monotone which are the signature of a bad interview.

Interviewing George Clooney is the opposite of a one-night stand. He makes an effort to connect, and likes to turn around a question and throw it back to you, putting you on your guard. The first time I met him he wasn't the big star that he is now, it was when he was in the butt-clenchingly bad *Batman & Robin* – not his finest role. It was one of those mad set-ups where we had three minutes in a hotel room with a publicist standing at the door holding a stopwatch, but I floated away on cloud nine. Years later, I interviewed him again, in a more relaxed way and he was even better. I wonder whether he's so grounded partly because he wasn't hugely famous until quite late on; he was a civilian for his formative years. I also think that intelligence plays a big part. He is really very funny. I took him a crate of beer – although I can't tell you why now. He's one of the great sex symbols of our time, but he's not obviously flirtatious in a boy–girl sense, he's just a great human being. (Mind you, he did also once sign a card after an interview thanking me for 'all the sex'. Steve raised an eyebrow when he read it.)

Michael Hutchence came on the show in the mid-nineties, around the time when he'd just left Helena Christensen for Paula Yates. Paula was villified in the press, it was a savage and personal attack. It was as though it was an outrage for Michael to have fallen for a woman who was older and less beautiful than Helena Christensen, one who was married with children and ought to have known better. I'd loved Paula since the days of *The Tube* – and I'd always admired her vivaciousness and iconoclasm. Michael himself had a fearsome reputation as a rock god and lothario, but the person I met when he came in was quite different – he spoke very movingly about Paula and her children and far from being a hardened rocker there was a vulnerability about him.

Simon Mayo had always loved having bands play on his show – I remember hearing Robbie Williams and Travis perform for him – and I was keen to continue with this. Gradually it developed into a regular slot, which we dubbed the *Live Lounge*. My producer and I decide who we want in the *Live Lounge*, which means that we're genuinely excited about all the artists who appear there. These days there are quite a few slots on Radio 1 in which bands play live, but back then there was only Simon Mayo doing it from time to time and John Peel, who'd do things like having bands play at Peel Acres. So it felt quite groundbreaking. It's one of my favourite aspects of the job and it's become a hugely successful brand for Radio 1. The bands come in and hang out for pretty much the whole show and you get to see them together in action.

I hesitate to describe the Live Lounge for fear of shattering illusions – and illusion is, after all, what radio is all about. In truth, it's less lounge and more office, but that's come in handy. The first time The Killers came in, their drummer Ronnie improvised and used a filing cabinet instead of a drum kit. REM used a record box and Duffy's drummer pretty much used the side of a sofa.

Over the years there have been buzz words that get used to describe a special performance. First it was 'goosebumps', then 'goosebumps on goosebumps', then 'A-ma-zing' – currently the phrase is O-M-G! The idea is that bands do their single, and then a cover of a current track – the more unlikely the better. For me outstanding moments have been . . . 30 Seconds to Mars turning Kanye West's club track 'Stronger' into a rock odyssey, Embrace turning D12 and Eminem's 'How Come' into a heartwrenching ballad of sorts, Elbow having us in stitches with their comedy covers of Amerie's 'One thing' with its 'Gobble Gobble Gobble' refrain and their helium-filled version of 'Independent Woman', then breaking our hearts with 'One Day Like This'. And then, of course, there was the day Arctic Monkeys covered Girls Aloud.

It seemed like a great idea to ask the bands coming in to the Live Lounge to do something a bit different, so we generally get them to play two tracks, of which one is a cover. This has become something of an institution and it's brilliant to hear a band re-interpret a song that means something to them. The idea is that I don't know what the cover is going to be, so it's a surprise for me as well as for the listeners. There's always a great deal of discussion between the record company, the band, and our producers, and sometimes it's gently suggested that what a band wants to do won't work – I can't tell you how often we've had to say no to Dylan or The Beatles, because the idea is that a fairly contemporary song is covered. The trick is to try to get the act to 'cross over', to select something utterly different from their material and give it their sound – Arctic Monkeys covering the Girls Aloud track 'Love Machine' is a brilliant example. I loved Arctic Monkeys from the first time I heard them so when they were playing the *Live Lounge* I got on a motorbike halfway through the song to go and meet them at Maida Vale. They were gauche and awkward to chat to but once they launched into 'Love Machine', it was a defining moment when Indie and Pop got together. That day, that moment, I had goosebumps on my goosebumps. I'd put that in my top 5 favourite radio moments. If we have more mainstream acts in then we'll try to get them to cover something a little bit wacky. When Will Young came in, he covered 'Hey Ya' by Outkast. I remember that while he was performing, my team and I were in a total panic, thinking that it wasn't working, unsure where to look. And then the emails started to come through from the listeners and they absolutely loved it. Will was ecstatic – I remember him whooping with relief when he'd finished – because he'd done something credible and the public really responded to it. It became a big hit on the first *Live Lounge* album.

It's so easy to be critical of a band's performance in the *Live Lounge* and easy to forget just how nerve-wracking the experience is for the artists.

Alison Goldfrapp was virtually mute during our interview before pulling off a stunning version of 'A&E' and covering Klaxon's 'It's Not Over Yet'. Afterwards she was a complete chatterbox. Just Jack wailed 'Do we have to talk like this – I'm too nervous!' Half way through our interview before cutting straight to his cover of 'Live Your Life'.

Mark Ronson said that doing the Live Lounge was like doing your homework, handing it in to the teacher and waiting anxiously for your results.

Occasionally bands will do covers that haunt them – Biffy Clyro, for example, covered Rihanna's 'Umbrella' and had to put up with their fans chanting 'Ella . . . Ella . . . Ella' at them for a whole summer of festivals.

Jamie Cullen covered Pharrell William's 'frontin' and the two of them ended up working together and Klaxons did a brilliant and euphoric version of Simply Red's 'Fairground' ahead of performing at the Brit's and losing their minds.

Inevitably amongst all the gems you get the odd stinker – I remember Gym Class Heroes coming on a few years back and they were so laid back they were flat out. Their first mistake was covering an Arctic Monkey's track; Arctic Monkeys are really hard to cover because they're so distinctive. Their second mistake was not rehearsing it and the result was something of a disaster. Another time I had poison emails from all those Killers fans out there, when Daniel Beddingfield covered 'Somebody Told Me'. It may not be my personal favourite, but the point of the *Live Lounge* is to let people have a go and it's always way more fun to hear a band attempt the improbable.

Sometimes a band refuses to do a cover – Kings of Leon wouldn't – which was disappointing because I'm such a huge fan. But I do remember the first time they came on the *Live Lounge* – all impossibly tight denim jeans and facial hair – and so polite. All 'Yes Ma'am' this 'Yes Ma'am' that. But on rare occasions we do make exceptions – I really wanted them in the Live Lounge. U2 were actually heckled by the crowd when they played live on my show recently, for not doing a cover – they'd only told me at the last minute that they weren't going to, and Bono tried to placate everyone by singing a line from 'Blackbird' by The Beatles, but it wasn't what the crowd wanted to hear. Bono's answer was pretty good I thought: 'Then think of us as a U2 covers band.'

The Streets always refuses to do a cover, but Mike Skinner more than makes up for it because he's so open and such a joy to interview. I'd have him in every day, there are always loads of laughs and great anecdotes with him. When I first started playing The Streets, I was repeatedly asked whether I'd taken leave of my senses, but he's more than proved himself. A few years back, I was contacted by his record company and asked whether I'd be interviewed for a documentary about The Streets. I was outside the station giving a film crew my 'why I love The Streets' spiel, when suddenly Mike appeared. It was like one of those Jeremy Beadle or Noel Edmonds spoof moments. He was shaking like a leaf as he explained that he'd stolen a mike from Radio 1 and that now he wanted to return it. What I was participating in wasn't a documentary, but the video for the track he'd written, apologising for the theft. He'd taken it when I had him in to do the show in 2003, and christened it Silver. It was used to record his number one single 'Dry Your Eyes' and every track on the album *A Grand Don't Come For Free*. Now he'd decided to come clean, and written a song of apology, called 'Banquet'. In the video I'm looking really surprised – because I was!

Taking the *Live Lounge* on tour has been the most fun. It allows us such a personal insight into the lives of the bands. With Kelly from the Stereophonics, we did the show from his parents' house where he'd grown up so there were pictures everywhere of Kelly Jones, rock star, as a little boy; winning trophies on a beach, in fancy dress – just priceless because they all led to a treasure trove of stories. Same with Adele when we went to her place – we got to see the pictures of her as a thirteen-year-old dressed up as Ginger Spice and use the toilet where she'd plonked her Brit award to use as a toilet roll holder. For the Lost Prophets we again went to lead singer, Ian's mum's house, where all the mums had turned up to see their boys and reminisce about the early days, when their sons used to rehearse in the shed in the garden. Despite the leather, the piercings and tattoos, every rock star is someone's son.

At one point during the week-long *Live Lounge* tour one of the shows will come from my house. First it was Mika who came round – he came for tea the night before, with his manager, and we all played Mr & Mrs. Then, during the show, as we went on a tour of the house, he kept unearthing whips and various bondage items that had been planted by the one and only Scott Mills.

The next year it was Girls Aloud who came round and you can imagine the stir that that caused in our little village. Mum and Dad took on catering duties – my Dad desperately trying to fatten them up with bacon sarnies which Sara demolished, saying how it drove her mad that people thought she didn't eat. By the end, my Dad was on first name terms with Cheryl Cole – the envy of his drinking mates – and Jude was playing Singstar with Sara. It was like every boy's fantasy Christmas Day.

Gradually it came to us that there should be a *Live Lounge* album, partly because we had so many requests from people wanting to know how to get hold of Arctic Monkeys doing Girls Aloud or Marilyn Manson doing Justin Timberlake. We've done three volumes now and they've sold really well.

These are some of my all-time favourite *Live Lounge* moments:

Coldplay – when they were just starting out, they came in and played 'Shiver' and 'Yellow', and I fell in love with them all, so talented and earnest and touching.

Arctic Monkeys – this is my best ever *Live Lounge* moment: another of my all-time top bands, doing a genius cover, 'Love Machine' by Girls Aloud.

Elbow – I love Elbow; such a great band, and now finally getting the attention they deserve. They're a particular favourite of the *Live Lounge*; I've lost track of how many times I've had them along. They really rise to the challenge of the cover, turning it into a send-up. I've never laughed so much as on air as with them. The first time they came in, they told me that had something very special planned and they did: a cover of 'Independent Woman' by

Destiny's Child; fast-paced, ridiculous, hilarious. It became a cult classic and they found themselves playing it at gigs because the crowd would demand it, as far away from the UK as Japan. In the end they decided never to play it again because it was starting to drive them mad.

Foo Fighters – Dave Grohl in the *Live Lounge*, lights down low, singing an acoustic version of 'Everlong', one of my favourite tracks.

Robyn With Every Heartbeat – this went from being a dance song to a slow song because of the haunting rendition she did in the *Live Lounge*. A-mazing!

In the time I've been doing my show I've seen many breakfast DJs come and go: Chris Evans, Zoe Ball, Mark and Lard, Kevin Greening. Chris Moyles is reigning king of breakfast, though, and long may he rule. He's a sweetheart, Moyles; don't ever let anyone tell you otherwise. He and I get on very well – these days. He comes in to my studio for a chat after his show, and furnishes me a hug and the latest piece of gossip. But there was a Cold War period, and I'm largely to blame for it. I can be hopelessly shy and there was something about Moyles's on-air persona which made me very wary of him. It turns out that Moyles is a fellow sufferer, and we were mistrustful of one another in a way that only two very bashful people can be. I pretty much avoided him and so he, quite rightly, thought I was being aloof and unfriendly. Our daily handovers became more and more prickly and I think my continued failure to make any effort to communicate began to really rankle.

In the end it was Chris who made the effort. In 2004 we travelled together to Dublin on a U2 junket – the band was promoting their album, *How to Dismantle an Atomic Bomb*. Somehow Moyles got wind of my utter dread of flying. Rather than persecuting me, he chose to be kind and solicitous, in a Moyles sort of a way, by hurling abuse and paper cups at me and making me laugh. It worked. Then, in Dublin, we were treated to the most lavish spectacle by U2 – the band never do anything by halves. We started out with dinner at Bono's – the whole team – engineers and all. Then they played for us, a gig that went out live on Zane Lowe's show, after that we were taken by horse and carriage across Dublin, followed by late-night gambling and drinking with the band. I have a surreal memory of being in a casino hand outstretched like a kid, as Bono peeled off notes and handed them to me so I could use (and lose) them at the gambling tables. Moyles still takes great pleasure in reminding me of the size of my hangover the following morning, and the hatchet is now well and truly buried.

Despite my protestations about being all about the music, and dreading live performance, I do still do that stuff because it's part of the life of a Radio 1 DJ. There are things I HATE doing though, and which I've filed away as almost too embarrassing to speak of. One is learning the steps to the 'Soulja Boy Dance', an incredibly intricate set of moves to the track by Soulja Boy himself. My producer, Sam, convinced me that it would be a great idea for me to master the moves and post them up on my blog for the world to see. And laugh at. And oh how they laughed. I don't have an ounce of rhythm in my body; I'm an embarrassment to my parents, who are brilliant dancers, and to my daughter who can shake her booty like anything. I've always longed to be a dancer, but it eludes me in the way that the ability to fly eludes all of us mere mortals. What possessed me to reveal this to the entire nation is beyond me. Perhaps I thought nobody would bother to take a look, but they did – they watched and they talked about it on air and they took the mickey mercilessly. Which I deserved.

But there are also times now when I enjoy myself onstage. When I dragged myself down to the Little Noise Sessions last year just two weeks after Coco was born to introduce Keane, Matt Horne from *Gavin and Stacey* and I worked up a little comedy routine of which I was (pathetically perhaps) rather proud. Afterwards Steve told me it was pure *Morecambe and Wise* and I realised that that's what I'd had in the back of my mind when we were working out what to say – the Whileys were huge *Morecambe and Wise* fans. Another highlight for me was hiring a tank and driving it over Scott Mills' car. I suppose I'm relaxing into the spoof side of things – I've never taken myself too seriously, but it takes a giant effort to conquer the shyness and learn how to be a performer.

Of course there's a bit of history behind my decision to destroy Scott's car, he's a man who does bad things. One question I'm asked very often is, have Scott Mills and I ever had a fling? The answer to which is, believe me, I'm not his type, though we were caught in bed together in Magaluf. It was after the incident involving me, a probe, and the bikini-clad girl. We were recovering from the trauma on Scott's hotel room balcony, and being rather rowdy, it would seem. Hotel management came and discreetly asked us to keep the noise down. Then, when we got even louder, they stormed the room. In a fit of drunken panic, Scott and I leapt into his bed and hid under the covers, lying there, shaking with laughter while the hotel manager tried to make out exactly what we were up to.

I like to think that he does it out of love, but Scott has been waging war on me for quite a while now. One campaign involved getting an airport lounge – departures at Newquay Airport – named for me. I have my own plaque and everything. Unfortunately it made me a target for environmental campaigners, who see me as somehow endorsing carbon-emitting air travel by 'lending' my name to a departure lounge. Scott followed this up by getting a plane named after me – Jet 2 Jo Whiley, it's called. I found out that he'd scored this coup when I received a text from Ricky Wilson from Kaiser Chiefs, saying, 'I've just boarded a plane called Jo Whiley.' Then another friend of mine was onboard Jo and they had to do an emergency landing, and the oxygen masks came down. I later got a text from her saying, 'Don't EVER fly Jo Whiley!'

Left: My debut as a bridesmaid with my mum. © WHILEY-MORTON FAMILY ARCHIVE

Below: An early photo-booth shoot with Frances on our regular Saturday-morning forays into town. © WHILEY-MORTON FAMILY ARCHIVE

Below: Photographic evidence of my addiction to Elnett hairspray and crimper. © WHILEY-MORTON FAMILY ARCHIVE

Above: Where I found my heaven – behind the desk at Turn It Up – Radio Sussex 5.
© WHILEY-MORTON FAMILY ARCHIVE

Left: Interviewing the Chemical Brothers for the Lunchtime Social at Radio 1.
© WHILEY-MORTON FAMILY ARCHIVE

Above: The gang – Mum, Dad, Frances and me. Steve took this, which is why we're all laughing so much. © WHILEY-MORTON FAMILY ARCHIVE

Above: Steve and me, young and loved up. © WHILEY-MORTON FAMILY ARCHIVE

Above: George Michael, always a great interview.
© WHILEY-MORTON FAMILY ARCHIVE

Left: With Robbie Williams at Glastonbury when he went AWOL from Take That.
© TIM ABBOTT

Left: Frances gets to meet one of her heroes, Mark Goodier.
© WHILEY-MORTON FAMILY ARCHIVE

Below left: Jude wielding the mike – a sign of things to come, perhaps.
© WHILEY-MORTON FAMILY ARCHIVE

Below: Festival girls together – India and me in the mud.
© WHILEY MORTON FAMILY ARCHIVE

Above: Sitting it out at Glastonbury on a day when rain stopped play.
© WHILEY-MORTON FAMILY ARCHIVE

Above: India is unfazed by a mud creature at Glasto.
© WHILEY-MORTON FAMILY ARCHIVE

Above: My favourite Chloë dress – bought in ten minutes flat, cost a fortune and I love it to this day. © RUNE HELLESTAD/CORBIS

Right: Back in the days of the Evening Session, with the boys from Blur.
© WHILEY-MORTON FAMILY ARCHIVE

Below: With Bob Geldof, Paul Gambaccini, Justine Frischmann from Elastica and Peel.
© WHILEY-MORTON FAMILY ARCHIVE

Scott's finest hour came about when I was doing the show from Blackpool, with The Killers. They were being their most sweetly unresponsive selves and, in desperation, I agreed to do something I hate – get on a ride. It involved being lashed into a chair and projected up into the air from zero to sixty in seconds. I had a mike strapped to my hand with gaffer tape. I screamed and screamed and screamed in terror. This provided Scott with wonderful ammunition. The sound of me shrieking and moaning like Meg Ryan in *When Harry Met Sally* gets played regularly on Scott's show when he feels like tormenting me. India was mortified.

So far, all I've managed to do is drive a tank over his beloved car, live on air, while he listened in to the sickening crunches and shattering glass. And I shot him in all the right places with a paintball gun. And I bombarded him with water-filled condoms from a great height. I also arranged for a horse to be brought in to Radio 1 so that Scott could take a ride, because I'd heard that he was afraid of horses. This backfired rather when it transpired that he is genuinely terrified of horses, as he took one look at the beast and fled. Somehow none of this feels like enough. It's so not over between me and Scott.

In the past few years we've taken the *Live Lounge* on tour, visiting the homes of various bands or having them round mine – Girls Aloud came round for tea last year, and the year before that it was Mika. We've even run a competition in which listeners get to act as host. One of my favourites was when Noel Gallagher ended up playing at Ben Hayes' house in Stockport. Ben is a huge Oasis fan – this was the tenth time he'd seen Oasis play – and he was just delighted, which was lovely to see. About fifteen people were packed into his lounge, with Ben's mum providing a wonderful spread and making cups of tea for everyone. Noel played three acoustic songs, 'Half the World Away', 'The Importance of Being Idle', and 'Don't Look Back In Anger'. My favourite moment was when Noel showed Ben the chord structure for 'Wonderwall' and then sat patiently while Ben played it back to him.

One of my happiest days out on the *Live Lounge* tour was with Lily Allen, on a barge on Regent's Canal, where Lily sometimes lives with her dad Keith. Lily had just been in Japan, and she was wearing her dinosaur suit, which has been on many a night out with her since and has even been to Glastonbury. Keith turned up on his bike in a pair of microscopic shorts worthy of John Peel (just in time to see me slip on the wooden gangplank and narrowly avoid plunging headfirst into the canal), and made us bacon butties for breakfast. The show was supposed to be all about Lily, obviously. But Keith didn't stop talking the entire time – he'd be washing up loudly, calling things out, interjecting. The more I tried to ignore him, the more determined to be part of the action he became. At one point, Lily and I were chatting, and Keith produced a calendar and handed it round the production team. He'd had it made up himself, and it featured, for each month, nude shots of Keith and Damien Hirst. Lily didn't resent his performance in the slightest; she clearly adores him and was happy for him to steal some of the limelight.

It's funny how there are perceptions about celebrities that all of us accept; this person is insanely difficult, this person is an angel. When you're preparing for an interview you find yourself planning how you're going to run it based very much upon those perceptions. Jennifer Lopez has a reputation for being really difficult – there are seemingly endless stories of her demanding that hotel rooms be painted white, or checking out because her sheets aren't the finest grade of Egyptian cotton. So it was with a certain amount of trepidation that I prepared to have her in the studio. She arrived with her husband Marc Anthony, which I hadn't been expecting. She was radiant and beautiful and something about her softer shape and happy demeanour told me she was pregnant. She broke into the widest smile when I asked her if she was thinking of having children, but she didn't confirm that she was expecting twins until a week or two later. We seemed to chat easily and they were a delight, a normal, very loved-up couple. (The only thing about her that isn't normal is her beauty. She's extraordinary looking in the flesh.)

There are certain bands with a reputation for being incredibly difficult to interview. Beastie Boys are one of them. Zane Lowe is perhaps their biggest fan – I think he's waiting for them to ask him to join the band – but even he struggles to get them to say anything remotely meaningful. They treat the interview as a combative sport, the aim of which is to really mess with the interviewer's head. They're playful rather than nasty, but it's very hard not to sound like a complete idiot. The first time I interviewed them I was still doing the *Evening Session*; I was young and naive and I'd prepared a list of questions. None of which they answered with any sense at all. I limped away from their hotel room, imagining them laughing demonically in my wake, feeling like a ball that'd just done several rounds on the squash court.

Fortunately, I was a lot longer in the tooth and battle-hardened when I first came face to face with Russell Crowe. He'd just had a baby and so I'd brought him along a super-cute babygro – which he held up between thumb and forefinger and dropped from a great height without even glancing at, before settling back and more or less refusing to say anything. He was a different Russell the next time I encountered him though, engaged, polite, serious, charming. He even gave me a CD of his band; Thirty Odd Foot of Grunts had just released an album, which may have had something to do with his change in demeanour.

Victoria Beckham must've had more column inches devoted to her in the past few years than just about anybody else you'd care to name. But she does give a good interview. She's very much in control, knows what she's doing and doesn't mess about. She was there because she'd just launched her fashion label and so the talk was clothes based. She's tiny, very fine-boned, but she doesn't have the malnourished look of someone with an eating disorder. I was pregnant with Coco at the time, and she brought me in a pair of her fabulous jeans, which of course I could only have got two fingers into. I had to give them to one of the young, svelte producers. The subject that made her come alive was her boys – Brooklyn, Romeo, Cruz and David. What I was struck by was how funny she is, down-to-earth, self-deprecating. You can imagine going out and having a real laugh with her – although I very much doubt that the evening would involve lashings of cider and then peanuts.

I've interviewed Madonna many times. One encounter in particular sticks in my mind. She was very much in love with Guy back then, and seemed to have embraced all things English, and was head-to-toe in tweed and plus fours. I remarked on this new look and she happily told me that see-through shirts were a thing of the past, which was surprising, given that she's the woman who pioneered underwear as outerwear. Why, I asked her? 'Oh, you know Guy. He doesn't want anyone to see my raspberry ripples.' Raspberry ripples? It took me a while to realise that this was an attempt at Cockney rhyming slang – she was referring to her nipples. Another time we were chatting backstage at the Brits. I was a little bit worse for wear and feeling very relaxed. Somehow we got on to the subject of horses, and I found myself suggesting India and I visited her country pile some time for some riding practice – and then realised my error as her smile froze. It's always a mistake to try to cross the celeb divide. She came in and co-hosted the show at the time of the release of *Confessions on a Dance Floor*, tiny and perfect behind a pair of enormous purple sunglasses. She was utterly professional – her manager sat down with my producer the day before and talked through every aspect of the show so there'd be no surprises – and was engaged and interested in the music I was playing. She described going out to dinner with Michael Jackson and advising him to ditch the white socks and loafers when he said he was trying to work out the way forward for him. The sunglasses came off after about half an hour, and the chat flowed throughout the music we were playing: kids, fashion, beauty, exercise – we pretty much covered it all! People always ask what Madonna is like and I tell them she's lovely – balls of steel but friendly – with a strong air of vulnerability. I like her a lot.

Jamie Foxx also springs to mind – I remember being completely charmed by him when I had him on the show. He's a charismatic ball of energy. (I mentioned what a fan I was of Jake Gyllenhaal and he whipped out his phone on air, dialled Jake's number, and left a message saying, 'I'm on Radio 1 with Jo Whiley and she wants to shag you.') I felt we'd really connected but then, the very next day, on the set of *TOTP* he blanked me completely – a salient reminder that the process of a celebrity interview is an illusion and if you're not careful it leads to delusions. You're simply part of a process and it isn't about friendships, or at least it very rarely leads to that.

My number one all-time favourite interviewee? Jake Gyllenhaal. (He never did call back after Jamie left that message, sadly.) Not only is he drop-dead gorgeous, he's also very clever and funny and charming and a great raconteur. He's an interviewer's dream. The first time I had him on the show was less than auspicious, however. James King, Radio 1's movie man, a man who likes to moisturise and Kylie's biggest fan, came in to the studio while we were waiting for Jake to arrive. 'OMG! What is that terrible smell?' he asked, horrified. 'You can't have Hollywood stars coming in here with the place smelling like this – it stinks!' Stuey, my producer, and I looked blank. We couldn't smell anything. A quick search by James identified the source – Stuey's trainers. We got them out of there and I was sure Jake wouldn't notice because I hadn't. But I'd obviously become immune over time, because the first thing Jake said was, 'God, what the hell is that smell?'

I think the most nervous I've ever been before an interview was when David Bowie came in to do the show. I'd done vast amounts of research, and I was sitting there waiting for him to arrive. My producer Pat Connor had popped out to do something and I had my head down, reading my notes, when the studio door opened. I thought it was Pat coming back and so I kept reading without looking up. Then a voice said, 'Hello there, I'm dying for a fag, have you got one? Can I smoke in here?' It was the Thin White Duke himself. He'd let himself in to the studio and settled down to wait. And I hadn't even bothered to glance up at him! The thing that struck me the most about him (when I'd recovered my composure sufficiently to make conversation) was how extraordinarily down-to-earth he was; he'd come in without an entourage, wandered around, found the studio and then settled down for a chat. It, was one of those out-of-body moments. I was transformed back into the teenager who'd watched him at the Milton Keynes Bowl and now, there he was, sitting across from me, blagging a fag.

The closest I've come to suffering physical damage in the name of my work was having my shoulder practically dislocated by Mariah Carey. Mariah is the opposite of Kylie Minogue or Madonna. Rather than being tiny, as divas so often are, she is very tall. She must be six foot and she's Amazonian in stature. We'd decided that it'd be fun to have an arm-wrestling league for all the acts that came on the show and I was fairly confident I'd clean up. Mariah was to be my first challenge. I was a little daunted by the sheer size of her when we met, but I figured I'd still pull it off. She is someone with a fearsome reputation for diva antics, but she's never behaved in a remotely precious way when I've met her. I suggested the arm-wrestle and she replied, 'Bring it on.' So I went round to her side of the desk as she bared her arm, muscles bulging. She flipped my arm right over in seconds, and it hung loosely for hours afterwards. The pain was something else, and that was the end of the arm-wrestling league. I'd learned my lesson.

*   *   *

I remember questioning my interview technique when the diminutive Ja Rule was sitting before me beneath a peaked cap, and I leaned forward, waiting for an answer to what I thought was a pretty insightful question: 'Ja? Mr Rule?' His tiny head dipped a little lower. Silence, and then the merest hint of a delicate snore. I sat and waited patiently for him to wake up. He redeemed himself, though. We'd just started a tradition of getting acts to read Christmas stories, and so when he'd yawned and stretched, I asked him if he'd read *How the Grinch Stole Christmas!* I suggested that perhaps he was feeling a little 'tired' and might like to take it away and do it? I didn't think for a second that he'd get around to it, but he did – he recorded it in his hotel room and it was fashioned into a beautiful festive tale by the maestro Joe Harland. It's gone on to be a Radio 1 classic. I get requests for it each year. It ends with him, in that deep, chocolate voice, saying, 'Yeah, the Goddamn Grinch! This is the Rule, Merry Christmas!'

I've had two very weird birthdays on air. The first one involved my producer, Sam, telling me she had a surprise guest coming on, someone I really, really liked and that I'd have to guess who they were. Now Sam had a reputation to uphold – she was famously mocked daily by Chris Moyles as a 'cockney sparrow' in our handovers, she was karaoke queen of Radio 1 and in her own words, 'the power behind the throne!' So I trusted her – more fool me . . . I was very excited, and wracking my brains to work out who it might be. I knew Justin Timberlake was in town and I was desperately hoping it was him. And for the first few answers all the signs pointed towards JT – it looked good. However, when it transpired that my mystery guest had never been a member of the Disney Club and had never gone out with Britney Spears, I came down to earth with a bump. It was not Timberlake, but Timbaland, the rapper, DJ and producer. He was then brought round for me to chat to as my special birthday treat. He'd just flown in from LA and he was jetlagged and suffering from a cold, which meant he sat in front of me like a bull frog snotting and grunting throughout our entire interview, which was a series of one-word answers until someone from his record company told him how many people listen to Radio 1, at which point he perked up considerably, and decided to win me over through flirtation, which, frankly, was even worse. Finally the show ended, the mucus monster left the studio, and we fell about laughing uncontrollably.

The other birthday that stands out is 7/7, the day of the London bombings. I was on air when my boss came down and said that there had been a 'power surge' on the tube, but that we should continue to broadcast as normal. When it became clear what was happening we had to stay on air, but tone down the whole show, keep playing tracks but also broadcast what was happening to keep people informed. I was desperately anxious about the children and wondering what was unfolding. Would there be other attacks? It was a while before I could get hold of Steve. After the show had finished, I walked out into the street and reeled at the sight – it was eerily empty, there was no one around. We went into a pub and sat and had a drink. I knew I probably wouldn't get back to Milton Keynes, and I had a moment of wishing I didn't work so far away from home – my instinct was to flee, to get to where my children were. It turned out that Steve had organised a surprise party for me that night and that loads of people from my past were going to be there. I was sitting in the pub, drinking with my team in stunned silence, and I started getting texts from people. I remember Simon Mayo texting and saying 'Happy Birthday. Guess I won't be seeing you now.' It was then that I realised that Steve had something planned. He and I met up later that day, and spent the night down in London, missing the kids. It was the best birthday party I never had but, of course, that paled into insignificance next to what had occurred in our city that day.

'Changing Tracks' is an important part of the show – an appointment to listen at 11 a.m. every day. It's where people share with us a life-changing moment and the song that reminds them of that time. Each story is genuine and each person is spoken to ahead of it going on air. I don't think there's any subject we haven't covered; from alcoholism to anorexia, drug abuse and divorce, and many heartbreaking stories of the loss of partners, parents, friends and lovers. Inevitably there are some that touch a nerve and these are the ones I read with my nails digging into my clenched palms so the pain overrides any tears, which would be unforgivably self-indulgent. For every 'Changing Track' we read out on air, I know there'll be many others in the same situation who'll find comfort from the fact they're not alone. On some occasions, though, a story will be deeply moving and the song so mismatched – Mousse T's 'Horny' for example – that people will come into the studio and say 'Blimey! Didn't see that one coming!

My worst ever on-air cock-up involved me reading something out very quickly. It was prime time, 11 a.m., school holidays, so lots of kids were tuned in. I had to read out a text from the West Kent County Football Club – bit of a tongue-twister on the best of days. The next thing I heard myself say, cheerfully and with clarity – beautifully enunciated – the 'c' word – on daytime national radio. Bingo! There you go, tabloids – have a field day. Needless to say, it was open season after that – of course this set me up as a prime target, and I'm still getting texts from Mike Hunt and Wayne King. Now I'm completely paranoid and read everything outloud slowly to myself before I dare to say it on air.

Perhaps one of the least glamorous moments in my working life involved the plumbing at Radio 1. It's not a very salubrious set-up, in fact, I think people are surprised and shocked when they step into our hallowed halls and find themselves in a rather shabby bunker beneath an office block – we've been there 'temporarily' for about fifteen years. We routinely have problems with the toilets. Once Scott Mills was on air, ducked out for a pee, got stuck in the men's loos, and had to climb out the window and back in the window of the ladies' loos to get back to his show.

On another memorable occasion, I had the delightful Keira Knightley coming in. The morning began with people sniffing the air suspiciously, and it soon transpired that the toilets were blocked. The smell grew stronger and stronger until the whole building stank, overpoweringly, of poo. There was nothing for it but to evacuate everyone except, of course, that we had to remain on air. So I stayed there, valiantly, alone with Keira, who is thankfully robust and strong of stomach. People often say that Radio 1 DJs talk shit; that day I smelt of it too.

Keira is an excellent woman, and not just because she'll stay on air when the place smells like a sewer. She's great value, down-to-earth, funny, outspoken; everything I hope India and Coco will be someday – she's a great role model and a joy to interview. That day, she shared with us her Changing Track for the days she was suffering outrageous PMT – it's Shirley Bassey's 'Goldfinger'.

I have to mention at some point our regular contributor each Christmas, Ricky Gervais who always, always turns up for our last show of the year to help the festivities. As a committed atheist he manages without fail to try and disprove the existence of God despite my best efforts to stop him. Once we bought him a fish which he named Michael – a chubby little bug-eyed creature. He lived happily ever after with Ricky until his demise. Ricky Gervais has the most infectious laugh in the universe. Fact.

The last, most pressing question – why do I do my job, and what do I love most about it? The answer, quite simply, is, what's not to love about it?'

What I do now is the equivalent of what everyone does on hearing a good song – you want everyone to know about it. Well, my job's like that but on a larger, more surreal scale. There's nothing like hearing the Arctic Monkeys' 'Fake Tales of San Francisco' and playing it to your mates – my listeners – and saying, 'I just heard this, I think it's great. What do you think?'

Festival Lover

I was a festival virgin until I went to Glastonbury. It was my first, and it will probably be my last. Glastonbury is my festival. I first went with a group of friends in 1982, when I was seventeen. We didn't really go to see the bands. In fact, when I think back, it's the punk poet John Cooper Clarke, the inspiration for one of my favourite bands, the Arctic Monkeys, who I remember: stalking about on stage before a sea of people, his hair on end, intoning those mesmerising words. It could only happen at Glastonbury – an enormous crowd, silent and awestruck, listening to poetry. Van Morrison, Judie Tzuke and Aswad all played, but it's John Cooper Clarke who really stood out for me.

My friends and I camped, of course, and it rained, of course. Rain and Glastonbury go hand in hand, as I've learned over the years, just like cider and Glastonbury do – for me at least. We turned up with gallons of cider, a tent and a little camp oven on which we fried sausages. I remember heading home early on the Sunday morning, after a small torrent of water burst through our tent at dawn, flooding it and soaking us and our sleeping bags and our already mud-caked clothing. We stood on the platform waiting for a train, frying sausages on that camp oven. They were burnt on the outside and a little too pink on the inside, but they were the best thing I'd ever eaten. Sheer heaven. I made it back home to Great Brington, handed my mum a bag of stiffened garments, the mud set rock hard, and collapsed into bed. I was returning broken but unbowed from my adventure and I was jubilant. I'd felt the Glastonbury magic for the first time.

And it is magical, Glastonbury; that's the only way I can describe it. There's the beauty of the nights, when fires are lit up all over the hills, stretching out for miles, and you're reminded of a fairy kingdom – or the Somme trenches when the weather is really bad. There's the feeling that you've left your normal life behind and arrived in a mythical otherworld. There's that slight edge to everyone, a mood a little like Christmas, or school camp. It's essentially an enormous get-together, when everyone has a laugh, gets over-excited and then decides they've had enough of each other until next year. Glastonbury is woven into the national psyche to a certain extent. The crowds seem to grow year by year and the drama, mostly associated with the weather. The weather never ceases to astound me. I read somewhere recently that the odds of there being rain in the southwest of England during that last week in June are as high as eighty per cent, because there's a weather event, a sort of European mini-monsoon, which tends to occur at that time. But more about later.

We first took India to Glastonbury when she was fifteen months old. Steve carried her in a backpack and we walked for miles across the Somerset fields, amazed at how big the festival had grown. It must've been sunny that year, because I remember lying next to India in our tent with the stippled sunlight shining through onto our sleeping little girl. Can I name a single band that played that year? Nope, but I do remember hours spent in the children's field watching Bodger and Badger and becoming immersed in their world. India was obsessed with them. I was on *The Word* then, but I wasn't there to work; Steve and I didn't have VIP passes, and we had such a wonderful time. And it was India's rite of passage, the moment she too became a festival girl, because she's been to every Glastonbury I've worked at since. She goes by herself now with her friends and they camp, turning up when the weather gets too much, she runs out of money, or if there's a band we both love and want to see together – or if she can't face the longdrop and wants to take advantage of the best BBC perk ever: the toilet. She knows the place like the back of her hand – it's like a holiday camp she's been going to every year for as long as she can remember.

Glastonbury is as safe as houses for children, provided they're with a responsible adult. But it has its pitfalls even for the young-sters, some of them connected to the weather. I remember India appearing after a voyage out and about with Steve and tugging frantically at my sleeve. 'My boots feel yucky, Mummy,' she told me. 'Just a minute, India,' I said. I was sitting with the producers going through the running order of that night's show. 'But, Mummy, they feel horrible,' she said. 'Hang on, Indi – just wait – your feet are wet, that's all.' She fell silent but then couldn't bear it any longer and struggled to haul off her boots. I looked up in horror as half of the worms on Pilton Farm appeared, curling round her toes, and landing in a heap on the sodden ground. It's difficult trying to be nonchalant in those types of circumstances.

Another time the issue of the responsible adult arose when she was about nine and Anna, a lovely friend of ours, took her for a walk one afternoon. She came back, tired, and a little sunburnt. She'd clearly had a great time. 'What is hash, Mummy?' she asked. 'Where did you go this afternoon?' I asked, with trepidation. 'Weed World,' she replied happily.

I was first asked to present Glastonbury when Channel 4 started covering it in 1994. I worked it for a couple of years, and loved it, before the festival took a break for a year in 1996, to let the land recover and the cows stay out all year. Then I was asked to be part of the BBC production team when the festival came back in full force in 1997. It was the days of the *Evening Session* with Steve Lamacq and, although I'd done some backstage work at Glastonbury and the odd bit of TV work, I didn't think of myself as a presenter, in fact, I didn't really have a clue about how it was done. Jools Holland and Jamie Theakston were the professionals, as I saw it, and the BBC had decided to draft in a couple of oddball radio presenters (me and John Peel, who was in an entirely different league) to mix things up a little and help out the glamour boys. Jamie Theakston actually ended up helping me out – as a babysitter. Back then, before I blew it for everyone (more of which later), we had caravans on site, very close to the tent-city studios. I'd have India with me, and often she'd play in the caravan while I was working. One afternoon it was pouring with rain and Steve was off somewhere. Jamie offered to watch India for me. So I did my interviews and India and Jamie played with their Gameboys in the caravan. Every now and then I'd dash across and peer in the windows and there they'd be, happy as anything, absorbed in their Pokemon world, oblivious to the international rock festival going on around them.

That year, 1997, became known as the Festival of Mud – it was the year when torrential downpours just before the start caused massive flooding. People were being treated for trench foot, and the price of wellies rocketed during the course of the weekend. I'd never encountered mud like that before. It was deep and it was sticky and you'd put your foot in it and then be unable to pull it back out to take the next step. After the third such incident I decided not to replace the wellies I'd lost to the mud – it seemed easier to risk the dreaded trench foot. So I'd turn up at the studio barefoot, wary of muddying all the beautiful silks they'd swathed the canvas in, in a rather futile attempt to disguise our basic conditions. Backstage isn't actually very different to the front of house at the festival, even now, when things are far more organised. The toilets are perhaps a smidgeon cleaner, but it's never been the glamorous enclave that the regular festival-goers probably imagine. You still get the same amount of dirt and grime and the beer is still warm, which is why I stick to cider.

I'd known John Peel for a while by then: he was one of the

legends who were still there when I arrived at Radio 1. He very much kept himself to himself when I was first there and he enjoyed a status quite different from the likes of Simon Bates and DLT, because he was such a maverick, and because for him music was everything. Although I was doing the *Evening Session* then, which was all about introducing the listeners to new bands, I was so mainstream compared to John, with his avant-garde tastes and phenomenal knowledge. And I was too shy to go anywhere near him. But gradually we got to know each other. The *Evening Session* came before his session and so we had to do a handover each night – he was always gracious and bothered to acknowledge my presence.

Then his wife Sheila had a stroke, which she recovered from in time, but the impact on John was enormous – he was shaken to the core. I came out of the studio one evening with Alison Howe, now the producer of *Later*, but for many, many years, John's producer and right-hand woman. We stood in the street and he poured his heart out to us in floods of tears and I was overwhelmed by the depth of his love for her. So we grew friendly over time, but I didn't really get to know him properly until Glastonbury.

I'll never forget the day we began our Glastonbury coverage together. There he was, resplendent on a hay bale in mud-caked wellies and a pair of rather alarmingly brief shorts. I felt very much the apprentice and wasn't sure how best to approach John. In the end I decided there was nothing for it but to plonk myself down next to him and get on with it. At least he knows what he's doing, I told myself. I can follow his lead. I was expecting him to give me a rundown of how we were going to work – you say this, then I'll follow on with that. I waited for John to speak. Then the producer told us we were about to go live. 'So – what do we do?' John asked. I looked at the blank expression on his face and it dawned on me that he was as clueless as I was. My heart sank to my bare, muddy feet. It was too late to ask anyone else for guidance. 'Well, viewers,' John began, 'you find us in the middle of a boggy field at Glastonbury and frankly we haven't a clue what's going on.' He smiled at me. My turn, clearly: 'But we're going to hear some great music,' was all I could manage.

We were off – and that moment set the tone for the years which followed. John and I quickly bonded over our shared feelings of helplessness. Things were pretty different back then – makeshift and glamour-free. There were no stylists; just John and me in a sea of mud, on our hay bales, trying to convey to the viewers back home enjoying Sofa Glastonbury the excitement and magic of the place and our joy at seeing such wonderful music being made. We looked shabby and we were chaotic, but I think it's the happiest I've ever been on TV. I do remember one of the producers sidling up to me and telling me I had to do something about John's shorts. I was puzzled. What was I supposed to do about them? The producer indicated that there was a little too much crotch action and so it was left to me to ask him if he'd cross his legs. I'll be honest with you – it was an awkward moment. Needless to say, those shorts kept appearing on national TV. Nowadays it's all quite fancy – we have a mirror *and* a girl to do our make-up! I still have to play it safe though and hang on to my 'look', such as it is: wellies (naturally), pigtails and a cowboy hat to avoid the bad-hair scenario which every presenter dreads, and sunglasses. One year I attempted a more glamorous look after bumping into Gok Wan in a shop and telling him where I was heading. He did a supermarket sweep of a high-end boutique and I came out way poorer, but with a splendid clutch of gorgeous but impractical clothes. And that's how I came to be waiting to interview Shirley Bassey in the rain, freezing my butt off, a mac over some flimsy creation I'd bought in the hope that I'd be standing before the camera in dappled light at the end of a long, golden day in the sun.

I could never pretend to have John's taste in music, so I never tried to. It became something of a running joke between us. He'd head off to the outer reaches to see the Congolese musician Kanda Bongo Man and I'd be off in the opposite direction to see

Razorlight. 'You young people may find that entertaining but I'd rather pierce my eyes with a compass,' was his stock response. It's because of John and his zest for the stuff that goes on in the far-flung corners that I really got to grips with exactly what Glastonbury is about – it isn't only what's on the Pyramid stage and what gets TV coverage that is important. Glastonbury is the sum of its parts, and John made me realise that more than anyone.

As the TV coverage strayed late into the night, so we turned to our vices to help the evening pass more pleasantly – Jack Daniels for me, red wine for John – and with the TV screens playing out the bands' performances, I would sit there, hanging onto John's every word. I could listen to him talk for hours, soaking it all in as he ruminated about the state of music, goings-on at the BBC, telling endless, hilarious stories of past misdemeanours. Gradually, the format we arrived at on air involved me more or less interviewing him, because I'd grown to love him telling me tales from the deep dark past. I'd ask him if he'd ever seen the Beach Boys play, say, and he'd reply that yes, he'd seen them thirty years ago, just as *Pet Sounds* came out and then there'd be some fantastic anecdote about him and Brian Wilson, generally involving mad, bad behaviour all round. We'd just be talking like we always did, sharing it with the nation. That first year, the Festival of Mud, the weekend's TV coverage ended with a shot of John carrying me on his back through the mud, proclaiming, 'Good night viewers – this is the end of the world.'

Because, for the past twenty years or so that I've been associated with Glastonbury, the weather could mostly be described as apocalyptic, the times when it wasn't really stand out for me. One Glastonbury I hold particularly dear is 1995, pre-Peel for me, in the days of the *Evening Session*. The weather was golden, from the beginning of the weekend to the end. The Stone Roses were headlining and had played at the gig for the people of Pilton in the build-up. (Michael Eavis organises a gig for the locals to thank them, a group of people who have had the privilege of seeing just about every major act perform for the past thirty years or so, something which must go some way towards alleviating the potential irritation of the influx of over-enthusiastic festival folk each year.) Then, as the band began to fall apart, The Stone Roses pulled out at the eleventh hour and Pulp replaced them. They'd been on the *Evening Session* and I loved them – Jarvis Cocker is just fabulous, he's such a smart, fascinating man. He's one of those people whose quirkiness is genuine – I remember him wandering around the festival clutching a plastic bag the whole time, no doubt containing a priceless piece of vinyl. We interviewed him for the radio just before they went on and he was terribly nervous, it really was a huge thing for the band. Then they played and they pulled it off – they were brilliant, the crowd were mad for it, and their career was made. They were around for the whole of the weekend, hanging out, elated, celebrating for all they were worth, Jarvis leading the charge. It was a triumph.

I was doing a bit of the Channel 4 presenting that weekend and we had a 'studio' set up in a bus backstage and we were able to do all the things people imagine doing when they buy their Glastonbury tickets: getting a little bit sunburned, watching something great as the sun set, and then sitting round a campfire at night. The whole Britpop phenomenon was in full swing and Oasis played that weekend, too. It was that famous year when Robbie Williams, the bad boy from Take That, had gone AWOL from the band and it was rumoured that he might be leaving. He turned up and appeared onstage with Oasis and then hung out with the band for the whole weekend, playing footie, smoking tabs, drinking beer and being a 'real' boy, having a laugh. Late one night, when the sun had gone down, we sat around outside the 'studio' with Noel and Liam Gallagher and Jarvis Cocker, and Robbie. I have a photo of him which I treasure from that night, his hair is bleached, he's unshaven, smoking, a world away from the clean boy-bander he'd been. The papers were hinting that he'd lost the plot, but I remember thinking that couldn't be further from the truth – he'd made a big decision and, for that moment, that lost weekend, he was really happy because of it.

Early on in our Glastonbury days, I confided in John that I was pregnant with Jude – I probably felt the need to explain why I was going easy on the cider. I hadn't told anyone else yet, not even Mum and Dad, only Steve and I knew. But I found myself telling John and his response was just so lovely. He told me then and there how much he and Sheila had wanted more children (they had four), but that it wasn't to be. And from then on, we'd talk endlessly about family. I've never known anyone so in love with their spouse as John was with his wife – utterly besotted. Years before I met him I'd heard him referring to her as 'the Pig' on the radio and thought it sounded a bit wrong. But then, when I got to know him, he told me how she snorted when she laughed, like a pig, hence the nickname. I feel as though I partly owe it to him that Steve and I have ended up with four children. He made it seem so easy. There they'd all be, lined up like ducklings watching as we did our shows. He helped me to realise that you could be in the public eye in the music industry and be quite open about having children; that they didn't have to be hidden away – that children are there to be celebrated. I asked him for parenting advice so many times and I so wish he were still here as my kids grow up as I'd give anything to hear the advice of someone who's lived a rock 'n' roll lifestyle and yet managed to raise four children as fabulous as his – they're such a credit to him and Sheila – I just wish he'd left behind a rule book for me. John also helped me to find my way as a presenter. Knowing him made me see that you don't have to have a radio persona, that it's possible to succeed and just be yourself, unadorned, and that you can be a Radio 1 DJ and hold true to your musical beliefs. Anyone who ever listened to *Home Truths* on Radio 4 will know that John was utterly honest and so people felt able to connect with him and relate their lives with his, painfully, at times. It should also be noted that this honesty was displayed in a number of ways – for one, he could be spectacularly grumpy and downbeat, and never masked his irritation with people or technology. There are some priceless recordings of John playing records at the wrong speed and grumbling bitterly about the equipment as he attempted to put things right.

It was such a terrible shock for everyone when he died. I had a sense that I've only had once before in my lifetime, with the death of Diana, Princess of Wales, of a nation in mourning. And it was made all the more bizarre because I knew how John would've reacted to it: he would've been rather embarassed by all the fuss. It was so unexpected and so odd, because John hated going on holiday, hated flying more than I do, but he'd finally decided he needed a break and so he and Sheila were in Peru when he collapsed and died. I'll never forget the funeral in the gorgeous cathedral at Bury St Edmunds. The family chose not to separate friends and family from fans, so the public were encouraged to turn up to the funeral rather than a later memorial service. It was a great, egalitarian thing to do and so perfect for John. He treated his fans as friends, after all. More than two thousand people turned up, and there were crowds outside listening to the speeches. Inside were so many people from his past: Jarvis Cocker, Robert Plant, Billy Bragg, Fergal Sharkey. It was as if Glastonbury had gone to church. I remember that we were all seated when two figures walked in, dressed in black: the White Stripes. I knew how moved John would've been by that – he'd championed them from very early on and his passion for finding raw talent was always an inspiration to me. I'll never forget the moment that the opening bars of 'Teenage Kicks' by The Undertones rang out in the cathedral, all of us crying and laughing at the same time as John's all-time favourite track echoed around the vast space.

The Glastonbury following John's death, 2005, was apocalyptic in its vile weather. It was so awful that I couldn't help seeing it as some weather god in mourning for John, or John up there some-where, playing an elaborate joke on us. It really was beyond bad, that mini-monsoon hit with a vengeance, and the mud was knee-deep in places. And it was cold, too, not just wet – more like November than June. It was so strange to be there without John. It's still strange and I still miss him all the time, but that year was the worst. There was a freak weather event on the Friday – a once-in-a-century occurrence, we were told – when two months' worth of rain fell in just a few hours. Tents pitched on the slopes literally slid down the hill in the deep flood waters which became a soup of odd wellies, sleeping bags, and camping gear. And then the lightning struck. I was about to go on-air to do my show, taking over from Chris Moyles who'd been doing *the Breakfast Show*. Kaiser Chiefs were with us, getting ready for their performance and I launched into my opening link. Imagine my horror when the engineer drew his finger across his throat just as I began speaking. We were off-air and all I'd managed was half a word. While the technicians battled to put something together, the flood waters rose. I stood there in the water, occasionally calling in by mobile to give weather reports to Chris who was left holding the fort back in London. At one point I looked across at one of our brilliant engineers, who was standing waist-deep in water, holding an enormous knot of cables over his head and wondered if he got paid danger money, for surely it was only a matter of time before we were all electrocuted. I realised there was nothing I could do. Chris was doing a valiant job back at base and we'd just have to wait. Right at that moment Ricky Wilson, the lead singer of Kaiser Chiefs, ever the gent, appeared at my side with an umbrella and we headed out for a 'wade' in the murky waters.

Eventually the waters subsided and our line was restored. Kaiser Chiefs never got to play, but I came back on air, the skies cleared and Glastonbury surged on, without John Peel, but with a firm sense of his presence there, which it always will have for me, as for so many other Glasto veterans.

* * *

These days it's all a bit more high-tech, as I've said. We TV presenters go down to the stage areas to film, but we often go up to the top of the festival, by Michael Eavis's Abbey Farm, to do our live links. We have to get there really quickly and so there are 4x4s to drive us round and get up the slopes in the mud. You'll be down at the bottom, in the tent city, and then suddenly you'll get the word that you need to be up at the top, by the farm. It's an incredibly perilous journey, not for us in the car but for the festival-goers. We'll have 0.5 seconds in which to get up the hill and so the driver has to get there as quickly as they can and there are hundreds and hundreds of people to be navigated around. Of course, they all hate you because it's raining and they're wet and outside and you're in a car spraying mud and water over them. I often find myself grinning slightly maniacally at the punters, who are shouting abuse and giving you the finger. I have to resist the urge to lie down in the back. And then there are all the people who are too drunk to move or stuck in mud and not getting out of the way. We all just sit there, mortally embarrassed, thinking, 'Please, God, just don't let us kill or maim someone.'

Last year, pregnant with Coco and so shacked up in a rather cosy hotel off-site, I had a little more time to myself. India and I did something we'd never done before and doing it made me feel close to John all over again. We set off on a voyage of exploration, discovering the outer reaches of fields I'd never seen, watching performers, and trying weird and wonderful food, experiencing the festival in a much more rounded way. Towards sunset we found a 'wishing tree' covered in tiny notes, each bearing someone's heartfelt wish. These ranged from: 'I wish you were still here' to 'I wish I had invented the foldable wheelbarrow', 'I wish I had a bigger willy', 'I wish I'd known my mother'. I stood there reading them all and thinking of John and then of my two daughters – one on the brink of womanhood and one yet to be born – and I wrote down a wish for them both. It was a very poignant moment. We wandered through the healing fields in the dusk, and watched people lighting Chinese paper lanterns which flared up into the sky. And when the sun finally disappeared behind the hills, hundreds of people cheered and clapped. It was a truly enchanted Glastonbury moment and reminded me of a classic John incident when he came back to the studio after one of his regular forays to the craft field, clutching a strange-looking hunk of wood. 'I bought this for Sheila – isn't it wonderful? Look at the craftmanship,' he told me, his voice filled with excitement and pleasure at the thought of handing over this precious gift to his wife. Later, one of the producers described Sheila's look of horror as this love token was offered up to her. But that was John.

I'm such a fan of Glastonbury that going to other festivals almost seems disloyal. But Reading is my second festival love, and I've been going there almost as long as I have been going to Glastonbury. Reading is very different from Glastonbury; even before it was huge, it was very much an industry festival, and its focus was solely musical. My first visits date back to my early days in the music industry, when I was working at Planet 24 on the ill-fated *Club X*. I was very much on the fringes of the music scene, an onlooker who desperately wanted to be a part of something. Band promoter Scott Piering, who is one of the people I'd count as a mentor, picked me up and drove me to Reading to watch The Sugarcubes and New Order. I'd never seen anything like The Sugarcubes – the band Björk was in before her solo career; weird Icelandic synth pop. I remember being absolutely transfixed by her voice, the rawness and fragility of it, and their stage presence, which was enormous. I was a huge New Order fan, too, and suddenly I was not only watching these bands play live but also infiltrating the arcane world of the backstage area. It was a young music fan's heaven: artists to spot, journalists to lig with, it was a world away from my first time at Glastonbury. I was there as someone in the music industry – albeit a tiny minnow in a very large pond. Scott introduced me to anyone and everyone, and for a few hours, as Scott went about his business, I worked that backstage bar – watching the bands and making new friends – until I rewarded Scott's kindness and generosity by being sick behind the bar tent. Scott had to take me home.

I was at Reading with India as a six-month-old baby when Nirvana played one of their very last gigs in that backstage area, I wasn't drunk this time, but looking after my baby daughter. That gig has become the stuff of legend. Kurt Cobain came on in a wheelchair and within months he'd committed suicide. I remember reading the music industry bible, *NME*, the following week, which hailed the gig as one of the greatest all-time spectacles, and feeling utterly frustrated at having missed out.

However in 1995 I saw Foo Fighters play at Reading. It was an unannounced gig in a tiny white tent, set away from the main stage. In spite of the band's attempts to keep the whole thing very low-key, rumours had spread that it would be the first performance by Dave Grohl's new band following the demise of Nirvana. By the time the band got onstage, there was no room for another ounce of flesh and the organisers were in a state of panic. That gig was crazy and sweaty and utterly frenzied. The band had to stop again and again to ask the crowd to move back and give people at the front space, to let them breathe. At one point the whole gig ground to a halt as Dave pleaded with a fan to climb down from the very top of the tent pole before he slid to his death. When we left, ears ringing, drenched in sweat, we all knew we'd been witness to something extraordinary – the birth of what would become a stadium-filling, JD-swilling rock band.

The boys didn't go to Glastonbury until quite recently, when they could retreat to the Whiley-Morton caravan when the going got too muddy. Their first festival was Reading. India always took everything in her stride, perhaps because she started so early, but looking back I think the boys weren't ready when I took them to

Reading. We were on the side of the stage, watching Razorlight and Cass had his head buried in my lap. Jude was furiously angry, and had his fingers stuffed in his ears, shouting 'I hate this band! I want to go.' Dave Grohl was there with his sister. He decided to try to cheer Jude up and so he pulled his scariest face and stuck out his tongue. Whereupon Jude burst into tears and I had to bundle him away. He still refers to Dave – commonly known as the nicest man in rock – as 'that horrible man from the Food Fighters'.

I've broadcast my show from Reading many times over the years. Sometimes we try a different angle to get the audience at home excited about the upcoming festival. One year we ran a competition. The winners were to come with me to the festival, in a tour bus, and stay with me while I did the show. One of the producers, Will Kinder, came up with the idea to make a film entitled *The Real Jo Whiley*. The idea was to have me being sweet and loving with the four girls who'd won and then be a complete bitch behind their backs. I have to say I really got into my role as festival diva – it came surprisingly easy – telling them to shut up, making furious calls to my manager (i.e. Steve) about having to sleep on the bus with them, and then 'on camera' saying what a great time we'd had. In theory, all good; however, it all backfired big time – it seems I'm just a little too convincing as a spoilt diva, and people didn't realise it was a spoof. The clip is still there on YouTube and each year, as Reading approaches, I start getting emails from people telling me they know what I'm really like . . .

I DJed at the Phoenix Festival a few years running, which nearly killed me. As I've said, I'm not a performer. Being in front of a huge crowd and selecting tracks is my idea of hell. You're there on the main stage, playing tracks in between acts. If the crowd really respond to something you are momentarily elated, but then what's next – and if they all shift their feet and start heading off to find the loos, then you feel like committing suicide. And you're also aware all the time of the bands back there waiting to go on, listening. You're wondering whether they're going to want to kill you for playing a particular track just before they come on, you're trying to build the audience up to hearing a particular sort of music and that can be incredibly hard to get right. Some Radio 1 DJs really get off on it; they're at home in front of the crowd – Zane Lowe is an incredible live DJ and in demand by all the big acts – Killers, Foos, Muse, King's of Leon and it really is quite facinating seeing all the acts just before they go on. I don't see it at Glastonbury because I'm either presenting or I'm at the side of the stage rather than actually backstage. I've seen it in miniature at the Little Noise Sessions, but the whole phenomenon of pre-performance angst is writ large at a festival.

What I've come to realise is that most acts do something akin to praying, whether they're actually speaking to God or not. I'll never forget seeing Dallas act The Polyphonic Spree. They describe themselves as a 'choral symphonic rock group' and they are a ten-person choir, dressed in white robes, plus a huge band of about fifteen. They're slightly shrouded in mystery and they've been described as being cult-like; and they go into a sort of trance before they go on, like something you might see at an evangelical gathering. They huddle, they chant, they shout and, by the time they run on, they're in a state of ecstasy which the crowd imme-diately feels. It's really quite freaky.

Other bands really feel the nerves, something which I can completely relate to. Ricky from Kaiser Chiefs throws up pretty much every time. I remember interviewing him at Glastonbury and mid-sentence he said, 'Hold on a minute,' and dashed off to be sick. He came back looking decidedly green and I found myself giving him a nice back rub once the interview was finished. Most bands go into a sort of huddle, The Wombats do a huddle and a pep talk – God only knows what's said, I've never been close enough. The best entrance I've seen has to be those doyens of cool, the White Stripes. The band is only ever dressed in red, white or black. They were playing at a Radio 1 *Big Weekend* – it was a big promotional thing for their album, *Elephant*. They're really careful about detail; visuals are a huge part of their perform-ance. Their roadies are extraordinary to see because they have on a sort of White Stripes costume, too – ties, bowler hats, jackets with brass buttons, all immaculate and black and red and white. At the *Big Weekend*, the White Stripes bus pulled up by the walkway up onto the stage area, but the entire entourage remained on the bus until just before the band were due to go on. Then the roadies all came off, one by one, bowler-hatted and suited, and lugging drum kits and guitars. Meg and Jack White waited in the bus until everything was set up and then they stalked off the bus and played this extraordinary, electric gig. As the crowd roared for more, Meg and Jack walked from the stage straight onto their bus, which had its engine running, and must have gone within two minutes. It really was such a brilliant spectacle, from beginning to end.

There are two things people always ask me about Glastonbury. The first is, what is my favourite ever performance? It's hard to decide – so many great moments, so many extraordinary memo-ries. But if I had to choose one, it'd be Coldplay headlining in 2002. A few years earlier, I was given a CD by a record plugger for a song called 'Shiver'. 'You have to listen to this,' he told me. 'They're special.' As a DJ you get used to being told that every-thing is 'special'. You grow immune to it, but at the same time I always try to listen to what I'm given, because how else would I get the chance to discover really amazing new acts? This was one of those times. I knew the plugger was right when I put the CD on in the car. This band was good – and I mean really good. Chris Martin's voice was very unusual, powerful and yet so fragile you'd think it might break, and they were all clearly such accomplished musicians. I couldn't quite believe the quality of what I was hearing. So I decided I'd try to go and see them and soon afterwards I got wind of the fact that they were playing nearby in Northhampton, the support act to a band that *NME* were promoting. Dad loves going to see bands, so I took him along with me. The gig turned out to be in a tiny pub with about thirty people in the audience. They played a great set; Chris is a terrific showman and the band gave it everything they had. At one point Chris caught sight of Dad standing there watching and asked if he'd get up on stage and help out on the harmonica. Dad turned down the offer, something he regrets to this day, not that that stops him from dining out on the tale of Chris Martin asking him to join Coldplay. After the gig we went backstage and met them. I could see that star quality in Chris as soon as I met him. It's hard to describe exactly what I mean by that – a sort of otherworldly aura which Michael Stipe has, as does Bono. Chris is a fascinating bundle of contradictions – he has a shyness and vulnerability which contrasts with the performer in him, the larger-than-life personality who's full of jokes and biting wit. I knew then and there that I wanted to get them on to the *Live Lounge*, even though it was a bit of a punt as they were unknown. I don't think anyone can or should claim to have 'discovered' a band or solo artist, but there are some bands which I'm proud to have been associated with from early on in their career and Coldplay is one. Over the years they've become real friends too, something that doesn't happen often in my world. To most acts, no matter how much we get on when we get together, I'm just like the radio plugger, a cog in the wheel, and that's fine with me. That's exactly what I am, and I don't expect the fact that we seem to connect to mean that great friendship will ensue. But like all friendships, it's lovely and special when it does happen. They know all the family now, and Chris always asks after my dad. (I've also met Chris's mum, who, when she found out I was pregnant with Coco, clasped my hand and implored me to play Mozart to my unborn child. That's what she'd done with Chris, apparently, and given how he turned out, I wish I'd listened to her.)

Dad is something of a personality on the music circuit these days. It's surprising how many big acts ask me how he's getting on or seem disappointed if he's not backstage with me. I'll never forget being backstage with him at another Coldplay gig, and Madonna was there as a friend of Chris's wife Gwyneth. Somehow the subject of Dad's role as my manny came up and, to my great horror, I heard Dad turn to Madonna and offer his services. 'Don't you worry, I won't lock them in a cupboard – well, not unless they're really naughty.' Oh, dear God – my dad's here talking about locking Madonna's kids in a cupboard. Thankfully, she could see he was a real card and laughed as loudly as everyone else. (Dad, time to go. No, *really*, I'll get your coat.)

But back to that great moment in 2002. Coldplay were huge by then, huge enough to headline at Glastonbury. I was really looking forward to seeing them on the Pyramid stage, because it represents to me as a festival lover what Wembley does to a football fan – the zenith. I don't often get to see the big bands play live on it, though, because I'm usually hard at work doing the TV coverage. But this time I was determined not to miss them, and so I somehow bribed John into letting me up off my hay bale to sneak off and watch. It's one of the great sights, being on the side of that stage on the Saturday night. The crowd is seemingly endless; it's easy to feel as though every last person in the world is there before you. God only knows how terrifying it must be for the bands to be confronted by that view. As far as the eye can see, is a sea of humanity, flags and banners waving, bright faces tilted up in expectation, a rainbow of colour and far, far in the distance, fires burning on the hills. I can't stress how powerful an atmosphere it is. And I watched as they came on, tiny figures beneath a meteor shower of lights, before an adoring mass of humanity – it brought tears to my eyes. I interviewed them later that night, after the gig. India was deeply pissed off with me because I'd sent her back to the caravan to sleep, barring her from seeing her favourite band play. So I took a punt and asked Chris if he'd go in and say goodnight. Chris burst in to the caravan, a whirlwind of energy

– still on a high after headlining the main stage. 'The babysitter's arrived!' he announced to a startled and confused India and her best friend Georgia. He then proceeded to read them bedtime stories for twenty minutes until he signed India's autograph book. He seized it and started signing with gusto – but not as Chris from Coldplay. Oh no – he signed it as a myriad of other stars – and each one with a corresponding impression. So, as he signed Robbie Williams, he became Robbie Williams, as he signed U2, so he became all four members of U2. He rounded it off with a poem: 'India – tell your mum/she's number one/really weird but lots of fun.' And then, with a flurry of hugs and kisses, he and Guy disappeared into the night to begin their Glasto celebrations.

The other burning question I'm often asked is, where do I sleep? Do I crawl into a two-man tent each night like a true festival girl or do I slide out of the farm in a limousine and spend the night in a luxury hotel off-site? The answer is that it's generally too tricky to leave the site at 2 a.m., particularly if the weather god has transformed Pilton Farm into a swamp and, in any case, I'm due back again at 10 a.m. the next day. (I did it for the first time last year, though, because I was six months pregnant with Coco and desperately needed a bed by the end of each day.) There's also, as I've said, far more pressure to look presentable these days, which would be all but impossible were I to make festival HQ a tent. I need a wall with a mirror attached to it, and running water, and an electric socket. Until very recently, all the BBC presenters had caravans on site, and this was incredibly useful to us Whiley-Mortons as we had a base close to where I was working. But – and this is slightly embarrassing – caravans are now a thing of the past for BBC crew. And that ban is largely because of me.

I don't really think it's entirely my fault, but here's what happened. One year I was given the crème de la crème of caravans, a Winnebago which had previously been occupied by Kylie Minogue. I arrived on the Thursday evening and it was beautiful, a lovely sunset, the place was just magical. I was with my producer at the time, Hannah. The woman who taught Kelis how to knit on my show and ended up going to her wedding. We've shared a hangover or two, Hannah and I. She is infinitely wise, infinitely bonkers. A real one-off, anyhow – I digress. The man who leased the caravans showed me around proudly and said that it was 'indestructible'. It had satellite TV, hot showers, a double bed and a Smart car attached to the back – not that it would've been remotely possible to drive a Smart car around Glastonbury. It was, in short, a mobile palace and became the place for my R1 team to hang out, watch Wimbledon, and nurse their hangovers.

The year before last, the plan for the radio show was that we'd stage a 'wedding' for two listeners over the course of the weekend. Two girls won the competition, girls who were just mates. The idea behind it was to demonstrate the diversity of Glastonbury – all the ridiculous and bizarre things that you can get up to. The wedding was to take place in Lost Vagueness, the field where there are ballrooms and restaurants. Lily Allen was to choose the bride's dress from the stalls at the festival, Mika was taking charge of the hen do at the roller disco, and The Klaxons were taking the girl-stag on a night of cider drinking. Amy Winehouse was there because she'd just got married and we were going to ask her for wedding tips. But inevitably, the weather interfered with our plans. The rain started falling on Friday. It was a deluge, so wet and muddy that we couldn't get anybody anywhere they needed to go. To make matters worse, Jude and Cass were there, with my dad looking after them.

There was only one thing for it. The bridal party had to decamp to my Winnebago. Pretty soon it was teeming – the Arctic Monkeys, Lily Allen, The Klaxons, The Enemy, Calvin Harris and Peaches Geldof, all in various states of chemical confusion. After a while, Amy Winehouse pitched up with her new husband Blake, who seemed terribly sweet and spent most of the afternoon chatting with Jude and Cass and helping them with their colouring-in. Amy and Blake were still very much at the honeymoon stage, and talked a lot about how much in love they were, and how great it was to be married. But there was a surreal aspect to my interview with Amy. It was before the world knew about their problems, but Amy would manage about three sentences and then her eyes would slide sideways and she'd disappear into the loo. Blake would then leave off talking to the boys and get up and go into the loo with her. A month or so later, Blake was arrested and remanded in custody, and his pictures were all over the front page of the papers and Jude and Cass would be pointing him out and saying, 'Look, there's that nice man from your caravan.'

Lily Allen was there in her dinosaur suit, still rather worse for wear from the night before. She and The Klaxons and Alex Turner had wanted to enjoy the festival in peace and so they'd got into costumes so they could roam without being recognised – a ploy rumoured to have been used by Fatboy Slim one year when he dressed up as Spider-Man to avoid getting harrassed. Some PR company or other had been handing out Barbours and Hunter wellies and so the rest of us were in a sort of uniform.

Lily Allen is a veteran festival girl. I'd first met her years earlier. I was presenting for the BBC with Jaime Theakston, and the Chemical Brothers were playing. I was backstage one afternoon when a pretty dark-eyed teenager raced up to me and grabbed my arm. 'Can you help me?' she said, and then launched into a monologue, still clutching my arm. 'You've got to look after me. I think you know my dad – he's called Keith Allen. He'll kill me if he finds me in this state. Can I stay with you?' I was about to go off to film a link. Steve was there with me, so I presented him with Lily and told him to keep her under his wing. He tended to her for the afternoon and, as far as I know, Keith didn't find out what his little girl had been up to. (She's since spoken about this in an interview, so I'm not breaking a confidence by recounting this tale of teenage misdemeanours.) When her first album was

Above: Some of the beautiful children I met in Ethiopia.
© WHILEY-MORTON FAMILY ARCHIVE

Above: Vernon Kay at Live 8, along with my travelling companions to Ethiopia – Matt Lucas and David Walliams. © WHILEY-MORTON FAMILY ARCHIVE

Above: Recreating a famous scene from *Neighbours* with Kylie – I was playing the part of Mrs Mangle if you're confused... © BBC

Above: Noel Gallagher and I have a laugh. © WHILEY-MORTON FAMILY ARCHIVE

Above: With the divine Natalie Imbruglia on the night everything went horribly wrong... © WHILEY-MORTON FAMILY ARCHIVE

Above: With Madonna – during her tweed period.
© WHILEY-MORTON FAMILY ARCHIVE

You'VE SEEN JAKE'S WILLY... NOW YOU'RE ONE OF US!
LOVE, YOUR SCISSOR SISTERS
THANKS
Thank you
Feel the Love
Paddy Boom

Left: The Scissor Sisters' autographs, spelling out exactly how I too became a Scissor Sister…

Right: Brandon Flowers from The Killers with me and wee Coco at Little Noise, looking like a lovely family unit.
© WHILEY-MORTON FAMILY ARCHIVE

Left: Back in the days of The Jo Whiley Show – Björk, Jay Kay, Karl Hyde and the Jude bump in my belly. © ATIT PRODUCTIONS

Above: The Whiley-Morton tribe, in my bed (as usual): India, Jude, Cass and Coco, just after she was born. © WHILEY-MORTON FAMILY ARCHIVE

Above: With U2, when they joined me on the show earlier this year, during my first week back from maternity leave! © BBC

Above: Girls Aloud in the Whiley-Morton kitchen, with Mum, Dad, Frances and the kids. © SAM BAILEY

Above: Chris Martin and Will Champion from Coldplay shape up at Radio 1.
© BBC

Above: Coldplay at Maida Vale Studios preparing to play in the Live Lounge.
© WHILEY-MORTON FAMILY ARCHIVE

Above: Why can't I look like this every day?

released and she came in to do the show, we were introduced, and we both laughed and said that we'd met before, under entirely different circumstances. I think she is exceptionally talented and I'm so fond of her – she makes me laugh a lot.

But back to that sodden afternoon in the Winnebago: the Arctic Monkeys turned up with all their kit, wedged themselves in somehow and played an acoustic set. India turned up with a big group of mates to watch them and Jude and Cass offered around crisps and watched *Doctor Who*. More and more mud was being trampled in as the weekend wore on. It was as though we were all in a tin can, God knows how many of us wedged in there, on and off, for the whole weekend. The hours ticked by, everyone had a really great time and, in due course, the couple were hitched.

Come the Sunday night, Dad and the boys had gone home. I'd done the final late-night stint on TV and I went to pick up my things from the Winnebago to go home. Imagine my terror on finding the door wide open and meeting a roadie leaving *my* van having just used the facilities. On closer inspection I saw that he wasn't the first and with an uneasy feeling in the pit of my stomach, I grabbed my case and fled.

In the weeks that followed my worst fears were confirmed. An edict came down from on high: no more Winnies for BBC presenters. The cost of putting them to rights was too high. An angry festival person had compiled a league table of the state of disrepair and mine was right there, at the very top. My Winnebago of Sin was parked next to my fellow DJ Edith Bowman's and hers was still pristine by the end of the weekend. It was a very public shaming.

Steve is, as I've said, a festival purist and he has remained resolutely so over the years. It's not only Glastonbury that we go to, or that he has to attend because one of his bands is playing. Over the years, we have been to just about all of them. Because of our jobs, the perks are there for the taking in terms of VIP passes and nice places to kip. But Steve is having none of it. And so, now we are six, he has come up with the perfect way for us to travel. Our very own caravan, ours to trash as we see fit. Not the most rock'n'roll of accessories, I know, but very useful. He towed it to Glastonbury last year, managing to crash it twice on the way down. The first was at a petrol station on the M4 – having filled up with petrol he asked India to direct him out. We have no idea what India was focusing on because it wasn't the caravan or the car they smashed into – cleanly removing the wing-mirror. Jude turned to everyone else and said, 'Guys – there's going to be a lot of swearing . . .' After exchanging phone numbers, they finally arrived at the site by mid-afternoon. They had a substantial wait to get in, but were at last waved through by security. Steve waved his thanks, gave them the thumbs up, and promptly took out one Land Rover and three security men. More swearing prevailed.

These days, TV presenting is all so much more slick and rehearsed. I still feel enormous nostalgia for the days of old. Once I'd got over the initial awe of John and our amateurism and cluelessness, it was actually a very relaxed way to present. We were pretty much left to get on with it. Now there are those dreaded car rides up to the top of the festival to do the links, and worse still, the links from the pit. You're in the pit below the stage as the crowd waits for an act to come on. You have an ear-piece on, into which someone is shouting, often inaudibly. The noise from the crowd is huge. The idea is to give the audience back home a sense of the build-up to a gig and the atmosphere, so we go around and chat to people in the front rows. But it's an incredibly inexact science, timing when a band will come on. You're told to start the introduction to Neil Diamond, say, and you start talking him up, and the seconds tick by, and he doesn't appear, you have to keep garbling on about something, anything, and then finally he does appear and then you've got to finish your sentence and wind up with a 'Neil Diamond' – whatever you'd agreed with the producers that you'd say just as the act came on – as though you had always intended to stop speaking at exactly that point. It is beyond nerve-wracking; but at the same time it gets the adrenalin going like nothing else and I always feel elated if I don't mess it up too badly. Neil Diamond springs to mind, in particular, because he was very late coming on, and although there was a crowd of twenty thousand, I felt as though I was running out of people to introduce myself to at the front. As his fan base is older and very dedicated, I kept encountering people with a vast knowledge of the arcane world of Diamond's oeuvre. I asked one woman, live on national TV, why she had a frog with her; her disdain was broadcast live to the nation. It was as though I'd asked the most stupid question in the world. Frogs and Neil Diamond are inextricably linked, it would seem!

The ultimate in heart-stoppingly terrifying TV, was, for me, working at Live 8. I remember receiving a cryptic email, asking whether I'd consider being involved in a secret concert. It was all very mysterious, but my interest was piqued. The event turned out to be Live 8, the biggest gig the world has ever known. Did I want to be involved? Of course I did. It felt really important to me because I'd travelled to Ethiopia for Comic Relief earlier that year with Matt Lucas and David Walliams from *Little Britain* and Ross Kemp. This was a really ambitious project, too. It wasn't about simply asking people to donate to charity. It was about raising awareness and encouraging world leaders to cancel third world debt, increase aid and deliver trade justice to the world's poorest countries. It was about attempting something truly radical – bringing about change to the entire economic situation in Africa, from the inside.

I was to do backstage interviews, but of course that meant going global – *only* going live before an audience of a billion people. The presenters were Jonathan Ross, Fearne Cotton and I. I was doing the interviews with the bands – including Madonna, U2, Scissor Sisters, George Michael, Coldplay – and some of the links from backstage. I'll never forget the feeling the day before, when I walked out on stage at Hyde Park, of sheer, unadulterated terror. The magnitude of what was happening was extraordinary – all of rock's royalty in the one place at the same time. I remember thinking that there was no way I'd manage to get through it without messing up in some way. My knees were knocking and my mouth was dry. But then, the next day, when it was the real thing, somehow the professional in me took control and told me to pull myself together, and I did, and it was fine – surreal, but fine. Surreal because of the highest celeb count of any event anywhere in my lifetime – other than perhaps Live Aid itself. I had a truly out-of-body moment when I went to the side of the stage to watch Annie Lennox, who absolutely rocked Hyde Park: she was amazing, a tiny figure beneath a massive screen showing footage of young Africans dying of AIDS. I was totally focused on her and only dimly aware of the people standing around me and then, at the end, I looked to my left and right and realised I was standing with David Beckham, Brad Pitt, Madonna, Stella and Paul McCartney, Bob Geldof and his daughters, Pink Floyd, David Gilmour . . .

It wasn't just us presenters who were terrified. I've only been with U2 twice just before they've played a gig; once at the Little Noise Sessions, when Bono and The Edge were just very pale and silent, and at Live 8, when all of them were extremely nervous. I remember Larry Mullen saying his teeth were rattling, Bono announcing that he was going to be sick and then doing an excellent imitation of doing just that, complete with very real sound-effects. They opened the show because they then had to fly to Vienna to continue their Vertigo tour that evening. They were going on with Paul McCartney, and I remember the Edge telling me that they 'didn't want to be the band known for murdering "Sgt Pepper's Lonely Hearts Club Band"', which Paul McCartney had never played live before. They were of course incredibly eloquent on the subject of Africa and totally amazing on stage – there was a wonderful moment when they released white doves into the crowd as they played. And I really enjoyed interviewing Madonna, who was very calm and told me that her kids were at home in Marylebone, but would be listening out of the window.

I'll never forget doing the opening, being aware of the number of TV sets tuned in over the globe, through all the different time zones. I was to walk through the compound, pointing out all the acts in various states of semi-preparedness. I was chatting away to the camera, pointing out this person and the other, and then I spotted Elton John, who had always been very friendly in the past. So I said, 'And here's Elton John. Hello, Elton,' to the camera. No reply. He didn't look up. 'Hello, Elton,' I shouted brightly. He just looked even grumpier, but still didn't look up. 'Elton?' I resorted to more or less tugging at his sleeve and shouting at the back of his head. Finally he glanced at me and nodded curtly without speaking. I felt about two inches high. A very public humiliation, that was. I think the tension got to everyone that day.

I always enjoy interviewing George Michael and that day he was superb, slapping me on the wrist for mentioning that he might be doing some performances soon (he'd told me he was thinking of a tour before we started filming), and then telling me it'd get more exciting if he let me keep smacking him. I suggested he tried Jake Shears from Scissor Sisters instead, who's more into that sort of thing . . .

The whole day was such a huge spectacle, and I think there were flashes of brilliance and moments when I was really able to take in the enormity of what we were doing – watching Will Smith in Philadelphia getting each city to say hello to the cameras, one after the other, all around the world, and then getting everyone around the globe to click their fingers each three seconds, to mark each time a person in Africa dies. Robbie Williams did a superb show, sending himself up, rocking the crowd, and referencing Queen's extraordinary performance at Live Aid twenty years earlier; Razorlight seized the moment and gave it their all, right down to Johnny Borrell's shirtless Jim Morrison impersonation.

It's something I'm proud to have been a part of, as I'm sure is everyone who was there. Did we change the world? Well, if we didn't make poverty history, we at least made a billion or so people stop and think about what was going on in Africa, even if just for one day.

So that just leaves my festival track list. There are so many wonderful fragments and memories that I find it almost impossible to narrow them down. But here goes – some tracks that I love anyway, and when I listen to them now, I'm transported back in time, back to a glorious festival moment.

Playlist – Festival tracks:

Scissor Sisters, 'Laura' 2004 – Scissor Sisters are such a great band. I first met them when I organised a charity gig for Amnesty International. It was at a tiny venue and when they played there were only a handful of people in the room. I was a wreck, running around grabbing people in the bar and dragging them in to listen. And they were amazing – they played with the same energy and panache that they've lent to headlining at Glastonbury. I knew then that they'd go far. After the gig, Jake Shears, as shy and retiring as ever in leather lederhosen, asked me if I wanted to become a proper Scissor Sister and when I answered in the affirmative he promptly unzipped his trousers and announced that, now I'd seen his penis, I too was a Scissor Sister. This was quite a useful introduction, as it happened, since the perils of live TV were laid bare one year when Vernon Kay and I interviewed Jake, who was gloriously clad in a crotcheted jumpsuit, and the whole thing began to unravel before our eyes, making all those viewers at home on the sofa Scissor Sisters too. 'Laura' is such a fantastic track and they really brought the house down when they performed it later that night – Jake still in that suit, which had somehow been pieced back together but could barely be described as an item of clothing. (Little Coco is already a Scissor

Sister without having undergone the usual initiation rite – just after she was born I received an enormous parcel from the band which contained a complete outfit for her, emblazoned with teeny skull-and-crossbones, a child's hot-pink electric guitar, and a CD of rock anthems for babies; the coolest present she received.)

Faithless, 'Insomnia', 2002 – I didn't see Faithless play live, because I was in the studios, but Steve took India and Georgia to see them. That day is extra memorable because the sun was shining, the sky was blue and clear and the crowd was euphoric. I'll never forget the way India's eyes were shining when I saw her later that day – she'd finally got the festival bug.

Damien Rice, 'Cannonball', 2004 – Until Glastonbury that year, I'd only ever seen Damien play in the studio. I've always loved his voice, with its fragile power. But I was just astounded when I saw him perform. He looked tiny, gypsy-like – elfin, even – when he emerged, but his stage presence was huge; this frail, solitary figure captivating the massive festival crowd.

David Gray, 'Babylon', 2000 – doing my radio show from Glastonbury is far from glamorous. The 'studio' is a caravan, a steel box divided in half, with the engineers on one side and me on the other in a space about the size of a single mattress, with my producer and dear friend, Ben Cooper, wedged in the corner. It's all very makeshift and slightly hilarious and it gets positively riotous when we try to fit a band in there as well. The place becomes like a game of Twister – everyone intertwined and piled up and yet still managing to make great music. A solo artist is less of a problem, but I'll never forget listening to David Gray sing his spine-tingling 'Babylon', wedged next to me, the two of us eyeball to eyeball. I literally didn't know where to look – deep into his eyes felt beyond intense, averting them felt rude. It was one of those moments, excruciating and exquisite at the same time. I'm always amazed – and truly grateful – for the good grace with which David and so many artists agree to perform for me, wedged into a tin can.

Elastica, 'Stutter', 1995 – Elastica's lead singer Justine Frischmann and Damon Albarn were so in love and beyond cool. They were Britpop royalty and Elastica were the girls holding their own against all the boys, playing great music during what felt like a musical heyday. Their performance highlight was 'Stutter' and fellow musician Anthony Glen running onto the stage stock bollock naked!

Pulp, 'Sorted for Es and Whizz', 1995 – another defining Glastonbury experience and a defining moment in the history of Britpop, too. When The Stone Roses pulled out, citing personal problems, Pulp were brought in at literally the last minute and were stunning – a performance I'll never forget, made all the more magical because Pulp were the understudy outshining the star.

REM, 'Crush with Eyeliner', 1999 – the band turned up in a helicopter, totally rock and roll, and played an electrifying set. After they'd played, I interviewed them for the TV show, and Michael Stipe was amazing and intense – he was in a complete trance after coming off stage. I have a photo of him kissing me outside the 'studio' (caravan) after the interview, which I treasure. He's such a complex human being: a global rock star with all the charisma that goes with it, but at the same time a total gentleman, funny, clever and self-deprecating.

Radiohead, 'No Surprises', 1997 – this was the year I met John, an Armageddon year weather-wise, but the skies cleared when Radiohead played, and it was truly a magical moment. Fireworks lighted the sky as this gorgeous song rang out.

Kenickie, 'Hey Punka!', 1998 – another year in which trench foot and mud wrestling were the order of the day. This fabulous all-girl indie-punk pop quartet were favourites on the *Evening Session*. They were so entertaining, and their lead singer was one Lauren Laverne, who's now a fellow DJ. Lauren and the band were hyped up and ready to go on stage – when they discovered that it had sunk into the mud. It was one of the relatively few times when rain actually stopped the bands. So they pitched up in our tiny 'studio' and hung out with us as we did the show. That was also the year when two stages literally sank beneath the waters and the poo lorry lost its battle with the weather god and switched to spraying instead of sucking, adding to the toxic nature of the water swirling around us.

Arctic Monkeys, 'Mardy Bum', 2007 – as I've said, India makes her own way through Glastonbury these days, with typical energy and style. I'll never forget watching the Arctic Monkeys, a band I adore, from the side of the stage, and looking up on the screens to see India caught on film, up against the barriers. It was one of those moments of recognition you have as a parent – I suddenly realised just how grown up she'd become. One day she'd like to marry Alex Turner, were it not for the delightful Alexa Chung, who Indi equally adores.

Paul McCartney, 'Hey Jude', 2004 – it was Steve who introduced me to The Beatles. For some reason Mum and Dad didn't listen to them when I was growing up. Steve's a huge fan and 'Hey Jude' is an important song for us – we named Jude after this song. As I've said, Steve is a festival purist. He likes to experience Glastonbury properly and refuses to take advantage of VIP passes. So I stood on the side of the stage and watched Sir Paul play 'Jude's song', crying as I always do, and knowing that Steve was somewhere down there in the audience, singing loudly as always.

The Flaming Lips, 'Do You Realize?', 2003 – lead singer Wayne Coyne was there all day, checking the stage repeatedly and counting costumes. That's very rare; bands often turn up minutes before they're due to play and leave it to their technicians to get everything ready. Wayne seemed totally on top of everything and so aware of the visual aspects of the performance. It was as though he was producing a huge stage show. And then when I watched them play, I realised that he was – it was a revelation, such an amazing set, filled with people got up as furry animals, huge balls being thrown out into the audience, bright colour everywhere. It was marvellous to see something so flamboyant and theatrical and so in tune with the spirit of Glastonbury.

The Polyphonic Spree, 'Soldier Girl', 2003 – such an amazing band to see live. The band and audience together went into an altered, trancelike state and there was a huge, uplifting sense of collective euphoria.

Rufus Wainwright, 'Hallelujah', 2005 – a great version of a truly great song. Rufus was as only Rufus can be – dressed in teeny seersucker shorts and being hilariously camp. The clouds parted and the sun shone down, and everyone was lost in the moment, until he forgot the lyrics and substituted 'Oh fuck!' right bang in the middle. Sadly stopping the BBC from broadcasting this song.

Jay-Z, 'Wonderwall', 2008 – there was so much controversy surrounding Jay-Z being booked for the festival last year. I'm a big fan of his; I've interviewed him a number of times. The first time was for the *Lunchtime Social*, nearly a decade ago. He was relatively unknown back then, but he had this aura of charisma and charm and intelligence. He's a huge physical presence, very tall, and very solid, but he's incredibly gentle and softly spoken. He has no anger; his speaking voice is high and childlike. Everyone was waiting to hear what he'd do after the uproar about him being booked to do Glastonbury and Noel's comments, and so, when he came out and did a cover of the Oasis song 'Wonderwall', it was a stroke of genius. It was a brilliant moment in the world of music. I was watching out the front and I stood there, in the crowd listening to everyone cheering and laughing, and knew that Jay-Z pulled off something really special.

Mother

India Eden Whiley-Morton – 1992

India was my first child and, for a long time, our only. She was a honeymoon baby – Steve and I were so loved-up and into one another that when I realised I was pregnant (and had got over the shock) it seemed perfect – everything I wanted, all in the space of our first year of marriage.

Steve is an enthusiast by nature, and I remember doing the pregnancy test and telling him it was positive one night in bed. 'That's fantastic, amazing,' he declared, before rolling over and falling asleep. I sat up for hours, thinking – was it too soon, what about my job – all these things whirling around in my head. It's such an enormous moment, realising for the first time that you are pregnant. And there was also the knowledge that (as with all my children) I'd have to be tested for *Cri du Chat*. Such an anxious time, waiting weeks and weeks, not being able to tell anyone I was pregnant, not quite believing it myself.

At about fourteen weeks we were told that the baby was fine. I can't imagine what it would've been like if she hadn't been. All I can say is that I understood properly for the first time what my mother had been through with that last, late pregnancy.

I went to the head of the production company making *The Word*, Charlie Parsons, and told him I was pregnant. I said I'd take a short maternity leave and then be back, but with India very much part of the scene. It's funny what a big and bold move that seems now, you still hear so often about women being sidelined when they announce they're pregnant, or returning from maternity leave to find their job has disappeared. You certainly don't hear many happy stories about women arriving back with their baby in tow. But Waheed Alli and Charlie Parsons were fantastic and I was young enough (and naïve enough) to have the confidence to just get on and give it a go. I had no idea at the time just how lucky I was.

Needless to say, I had a playlist for the birth all lined up – I think that the labour takes on huge significance with your first child, because it's such an unknown. With subsequent children, the birth itself pales into insignificance next to the enormity of looking after a newborn which you know will follow. As is so often the case with first babies, I was in labour for ever, it seemed – three days or so, followed by an emergency caesarean at the end. By the end of the first day the playlist was out the window – I remember shouting at Steve to turn the music off. But I know that I'll always associate 'Unfinished Sympathy' by Massive Attack with giving birth to India. Also Van Morrison's 'Angelou' and 'Moon Dance' and the Cocteau Twins – our music. And I must also confess to associating *Jerry Springer* with those first, heady days of motherhood. I spent hours lying on the sofa with my baby girl, watching crap TV. I loved everything about those early days, and to this day feel a special affection for Jerry Springer. We named her India Eden Whiley-Morton – can't tell you why, other than that I really loved the sound of the names together. How things sound has always been really important to me.

The only slight cloud on the horizon at this magical time was Frances. She has always adored Steve, since the day she met him. He's incredibly loud and so is she. He tells a good story complete with silly voices and ridiculous mannerisms and she laps it up. However he's far firmer than me and my parents; her tantrums don't really cut it with him. He accepted her as part of my life from the word go, but he's one step removed from her, he doesn't have such an emotional reaction to her when she's being difficult. When Frances was told I was having a baby she was beside herself with excitement – she totally adores babies and is incredibly tender and loving with them. When she first met India for the first time, she stroked her cheek with one finger and lowered her voice to the softest whisper – which took a great deal of effort – and said 'Hello, little baby,' before planting a big kiss on her head; however, as is entirely natural, Frances had to battle feelings of jealousy and displacement. She had been number one in my life for twenty-seven years then, all of a sudden, there was someone else taking up my time, love and affection. Combining this with her own desire to have a baby (which is something she'll never be able to do), meant these were turbulent times. Like a child, she was unable to control her feelings, which was difficult at times for the rest of us to deal with. But, unlike a child, she was physically big and strong, so the potential for causing damage was quite high, and as India was my firstborn I was very protective of her. Frances would be sitting in a chair with India nearby when her leg would shoot out, or her fist would be brandished, and we'd all swoop to remove the baby from harm's way. I can't deny that on the occasions she did make contact, I had to fight very hard to suppress the urge to give her a swift kick back. It's worth mentioning that it's impossible to discipline Frances in the usual way because it leads to a full-blown escalation of shouting, crying, fisticuffs and ultimately achieves nothing – believe me, we've tried every which way.

India probably got the short straw because with Coco there's very little threat of violence – instead there's just all-encompassing love.

When it was time to go back to work, I hired a lovely young manny called Dave (another groundbreaking move, I now realise). The manny would have India while we were filming, but she would be at all the production meetings, sleeping next to me, and then crawling about the floor or across the table as she got older. We have photos of her with all the props from the set – her little arms wrapped around daleks. She became part of the furniture. I have, for instance, a fabulous picture of her with Rolf Harris, a hero of mine, when he played on *The Word*. He's gamely holding India and she is screaming her head off, her face screwed up and her red, tiny mouth wide open. The whole set-up worked, somehow. I don't think I could've gone back to Radio 1 if it hadn't worked like this. And I think that the great thing about having had my first child before my career had really got going and when I was still young enough not to feel anxious about my place on the ladder (in fact I didn't really have a place on the ladder), is that I just felt my way through without thinking too hard about it. When I got the call from Radio 1, I already had India, so I didn't have the fear that most women have about how kids will affect their career. That's one of the paradoxes of being a working woman today – being in control of your fertility also means having to make big choices and decisions about whether and when to have children. I sometimes wonder if I'd have had four children if I'd already been a Radio 1 DJ before I started having them.

India is very well aware of the charmed life she's had and never takes any of the perks for granted. If she ever comes along to any of the shows we do at festivals she immediately ends up working! Because she's so calm and responsible she will automatically be given jobs to do, none of us questioning whether she'll come up with the goods. She simply becomes part of the team. She first went to Glastonbury before she could walk. She's been to Reading countless times, and seen just about every major act you'd care to name. Steve and I took her everywhere with us; we were an inseparable team. When she was about four, we took her to see Michael Jackson. We were sitting with people from Sony Records and someone asked if India would like to join a group of children on stage at the end, when Jackson would sing 'We Are the World'. She was delighted by the idea, and I thought it'd be quite funny, so we told Steve we were going to the toilet and vanished. She had a massive bird's nest in her hair, and was wearing a Manics T-shirt, baggy denim shorts and mini DMs. Steve waited for us, rather bored, and wondering when we might be able to make an exit, when suddenly Michael started 'We Are The World'. Someone nudged Steve: 'Isn't that India onstage with Jacko?' And sure enough, there on the gigantic Wembley screens, was his daughter. He looked up at her, onstage at Wembley amidst a group of blonde, angelic children dressed in their Sunday best – pressed dresses, crisp shirts, hair neatly parted and serene expressions. India was oblivious, jigging away happily, and she failed to notice Jackson swoop towards her, recoil as he took in her appearance and then quickly make a beeline for another, more kempt, child.

Jude Blue Whiley-Morton – 1998

I went to Radio 1 when India was about eighteen months old. I was doing the *Evening Session* with Steve Lamacq and there was an awful lot of going out to the pub after the session and eating peanuts and drinking cider. It was the nineties, Britpop ruled the airwaves, things were pretty debauched; it didn't feel like the time to have another baby. And Steve was very happy with just the one child. I remember that a lot of my friends were doing the 'normal' thing and getting on with their second child, but we just weren't in that frame of mind at all. And, in spite of what I'd said earlier, there was some anxiety on my part about my career. After all, I was still loving the fact that I was a Radio 1 DJ! And it was still very much a man's world. Things have changed a bit – last year, when we had our annual Radio 1 Christmas 'family' photograph of the DJs taken, they took a girls' shot and a boys' one, for the first time.

The 'girls' were still by far in the minority – ten of us, but that number represents huge progress. I'm a survivor, and I've had kids during my time there and not made a secret of it, but I'm aware I've broken ground in doing so, I know that. I'm not complaining; I've pulled it off, after all. But at the time I felt under immense pressure and it was a while before I dared even to consider having a second child. Eventually, though, I surmounted my fear and decided that I was ready – India was four, after all, and I now knew that I didn't want her to be an only child. Steve took a bit of convincing; he felt as though our life was complete with India. But, in the end, we decided it was what we both wanted.

My career was really taking off at this point. I was offered the daytime slot and this worked well with India. She had started school and was beginning to resent me going out every evening, because she wasn't at home with me in the day any more. I also began to do TV work and I realise now that this affected me enormously. Being a DJ is all about sitting in the dark, speaking as though to your fictional audience of one. But I dread doing live performances of any kind. Up to a point I was able to manage TV in much the same way – after all, you can't see your TV audience, unless it's something like *Top of the Pops*, and even then it's a studio audience; you can forget about all the people out there in their homes. But suddenly, and especially with *The Jo Whiley Show*, my Channel 4 chat show, I was being looked at in the flesh, as it were, by a large and critical audience. Things were written about my appearance, some of them pretty unpleasant. I'd always been a bit of a tomboy; jeans and DMs were my uniform. Now, suddenly, I was dealing with stylists, who ordered racks of clothes to be sent over for me to try on. The clothes would be the dreaded 'SS' – sample size, what in today's parlance is Size Zero. Model-sized. And, until you encounter these women in the flesh, or see the size of their garments (which would be about right for Jude, now aged ten), you don't realise just how petite these women are, how different they are in size from 'civilians' (as Liz Hurley once described us lesser mortals).

I found myself getting more and more anxious about my weight, in a way I never had before, although it seems to me that the pressure on women in the public eye to be thin has been growing steadily since the eighties. There's nothing quite like being unable to fit into teensy little garments, again and again, to make you lose your perspective. Add to this the fact that, once you are visible, people feel able to dissect your appearance, and be quite vicious in doing so. So the gym became an obsession, as did missing meals. I lost quite a bit of weight and secretly I loved it – eventually I was slipping into those SS garments.

Steve and I started to try for a baby but nothing happened. We conceived India so easily, it had never occurred to us that it might be difficult the second time around. But a year went by, and we didn't conceive, and somehow it made me want to diet more – my weight and what I put in my mouth was something I could control, my fertility, it seemed, wasn't. I can now see how anorexia nervosa develops – I was almost headed down that road myself. I managed to conceive, but then had a very early miscarriage, which was tough to deal with. All that relief and excitement and then the crushing blow, the death of hope, and the feelings of sadness for what might have been. I felt such a sense of loss and of despair.

Steve forced me to go and see a consultant at this point, and I'm really glad he did. We were both checked out by a doctor and I was found to have polycystic ovaries and there was talk of further investigative surgery. But still no baby. And the doctors told us to go away on holiday, to rest and relax. So we booked a holiday, heading for the mountains – and Jude was conceived. It's amazing the extent to which your mental state plays a part in these things, in spite of the fact that the act of conception is an entirely physical process. It's one of life's great mysteries. We went away and I relaxed, tucked into some wholesome meals, and realised what was great about my life – Steve, India, my job. Suddenly I felt as though it wouldn't be the end of the world if I didn't have another baby. And then it all came right. Obviously I know that things aren't so simple for many people. While I've had to go through the agonising wait each time to make sure that my babies don't have *Cri du Chat*, Steve and I have never had to go through any form of fertility treatment, and our troubles in conceiving were relatively short-lived. I will never take for granted how unbelievably lucky we've been.

We named Jude after The Beatles song, 'Hey Jude'. Steve is a huge Beatles fan and it's a beautiful name. We had Jude when we were still living in London and I remember leaving the hospital, stopping for a hot chocolate in Muswell Hill, and sitting in the car waiting for Steve, and Radio 1 was on. Kevin Greening was filling in for me, and he said, 'We thought we'd play this for you, Jo, and your newborn son.' I sat there, clutching my little bundle of joy and cried and cried as I listened to the full version of 'Hey Jude'. It is a memory I'll always cherish and so typical of Kevin. He was the sweetest, kindest man and it was a huge shock when he died, just so sad.

I wanted to call Jude 'Blue'. But no one in the family (Steve especially) would entertain the idea. Now, I've always had a thing for cowboys thanks to Grandad, and I also used to love the TV programme the *High Chaparral*, which had a cowboy in it named Blue, who I thought was terribly cool. So, when I went by myself to register the baby, I was looking at the form and a terrible thought came to me: I could name him whatever I wanted. I resisted the temptation to give him Blue as his first name, but put it down as his second. A few months later, Steve was filling out a form and asked what we'd done about Jude's second name. 'He's called Jude Blue,' I said firmly. 'Blue?' 'Blue.' By then it was too late, and Steve has come around to the name, thankfully. Jude just loves it!

*   *   *

My Radio 1 bosses let me take Jude in to work with me when I went back after three months or so. I had a nanny, Clare, who'd take Jude out to a café nearby, or have him in the studio while I worked and I'd breastfeed in between records or sometimes during the odd interview. (The second time that Christopher Eccleston came on the show, he told me that he'd been completely thrown on the previous occasion by the manny appearing halfway through the interview and presenting me with a screaming Jude. As I kept chatting, I'd taken the baby, whipped up my top, and fed him. Christopher told me how he'd been unable to concentrate on our conversation from there on. I couldn't quite believe I'd done that, but then you get so blasé about breast-feeding because your focus is on giving your baby what he or she is letting you know – loud and clear – is needed.) It was all wonderfully easy. We were so happy to have a little boy to follow India, and India was terribly pleased with her little brother – she was six when he was born and old enough not to be jealous. We felt like a proper nuclear family, all of a sudden, and I was happily absorbed in work and motherhood.

One of the fascinating things about having children is the way in which they have facets of both parents – physically and temperamentally – little pieces of the jigsaw that fit together to make an utterly distinct whole. Some pieces of the puzzle are so obviously from one parent or the other, some seem to come in from more distant relations, or remain of mysterious provenance. Jude loves drama, and he's often picked to do readings at school, at Christmas services and assemblies. Steve is much more of an extrovert, pragmatic, noisy, straightforward, sensible, and reasons things through. Jude is like me – far more complicated (I'm afraid to say), more intuitive, more prone to doubts and anxieties, but a performer like his dad. India and Cass fall firmly into the Steve camp. We'll see about little Coco.

*   *   *

It was when India was seven and Jude was a wee baby that we made the move out to Northamptonshire, back to my roots.

Dad was still working on construction sites at this time, and Mum was full time in the post office. But Dad's hands were really beginning to trouble him – he has rheumatoid arthritis – and we all knew that it was only a matter of time before he would have to give up work. So, in keeping with my return to the fold, Steve and I asked him if he'd be our manny. He agreed right away, so we were able to commute down to London every day and not worry about our kids.

Dad would turn up each day, take India to school, and then he and Jude would hang out. They formed such a tight bond, and they're still very close today. Dad doesn't talk a lot about his childhood, he never has with me, but Jude will often tell me something Dad has told him which I've never heard – the time he fell in a nettle patch, the fight he had with the boys in the street. I think Dad rediscovered childhood through Jude. They did a lot of trainspotting and watching videos about diggers. Dad was working so hard when Frances and I were growing up that he didn't have much time to enjoy fatherhood – being with Jude gave him that chance all over again. What they got up to each day was almost their secret, a world they entered together. And then they'd pick up India and the three of them would hang out in the afternoons until Steve or I got back.

Jude has already made a number of appearances on stage. He's partial to a bit of Mika, and when Mika came to our house when we did the *Live Lounge* tour, Jude was irrepressible. I'd ask Mika a question and before he'd had a chance to answer, a little figure would pop up between me and my interviewee, lean into the mike and answer for him. Mika (fortunately) was enchanted by him and by Cass too, and asked whether they'd like to come along and see him play at the Brixton Academy. Mika's shows are always a riot of colour and action and, at the end, he has a whole cast of dancers dressed as furry animals up on stage. Mika had a tiny Dalmatian suit made for Jude and India was a rabbit. (Cass refused to take part; he hates attention. Both boys love music – if they ever form a band Jude will definitely be the singer and Cass the drummer. He has the haircut, the attitude and a fantastic sense of rhythm.) The children watched the show with Mika's grandma, and then India and Jude went out on stage. India was mindful of the fact that Jude was still only eight and so she had him at the back, firmly by the hand. But as soon as the animals began to dance, Jude more or less shoved India to one side and careened to the front, where he danced hand in hand with Mika, leaving India staggering around with a massive tiger head, bumping into different members of the band – highly comedic.

Jude's other great love is the Mighty Boosh – it's got to be the most watched DVD in our house. He's word perfect at their surreal crimps. Our dog, a gorgeous golden retriever, is named The Mighty Boosh and Jude dresses for the most part like Vince Noir in skinny jeans and cowboy boots. When the Boosh were guests on the show, Jude came in to meet his heroes. Not exactly the shyest kid on the block, he settled himself down in the Live Lounge with Howard and Vince (Julian and Noel), while I got on with the show. When they came into the studio they said they were all talked out and had just given the best inter-view of their career. To a ten year old boy. Not a word of it recorded for us to enjoy!

Cassius Gabriel Whiley-Morton – 2000

Steve was really happy with two children but, in 2001, Cass came along without any fuss – he and Jude are just over two years apart. I'd beaten Steve into submission by then, and the third child was a done deal. We didn't struggle at all to have him, and this time I was really relaxed during my pregnancy, because Radio 1 were fine about me having another baby and I'd found it so easy having Jude that I didn't see that there'd be a problem with Cass.

Cass is the most laid-back character you could hope to meet. He's incredibly sunny-natured and self-contained, and he'll entertain himself for hours. He's really practical, and already he's the one all of us turn to if something isn't working – he's the one who assembled Coco's baby walker. I'd had a go, given up in despair, and left it in pieces on the floor. When I came back, half an hour later, it was sitting there, ready to go, and Cass was dusting off his hands with a pleased expression. I think there's a bit of my Grandad embedded within Cass. I found out I was pregnant the week he died and I've always felt he lived on in Cass.

Nothing fazes Cass. He's not a performer like his older brother and sister but, at the age of eight, he's shaping up to be a keen drummer – the perfect instrument for someone who doesn't like to be in the limelight. He loves The Police because of the great Stuart Copeland and whenever he's listening to music he'll be carefully drumming out the beat. We have a den in the garden where Steve works and where the drum kit lives. Cass doesn't like being out there by himself after dark and so Steve or I are constantly dragged out to keep him company for hours on end while he whacks away with his tiny sticks. He's named Cassius after the formidable Cassius Clay, Gabriel because it seemed to fit, and it really does suit him. He's angelic, by which I mean slightly otherworldly, an elfin child with an abundance of freckles – I don't mean that he's a model of good behaviour. He's mischievous and energetic and full of life.

Cass has always felt slightly miffed at the fact that his big brother had his own song – and not just any song, either. Then, not long ago, Foals appeared on the scene and released a track called 'Cassius'. I was so happy that Cass had his own song – until I listened to the lyrics: 'Cassius is over/Cassius is second best/Cassius is worse than less'. India and Jude took to singing the lines at Cass at every opportunity, taunting him about being second best, which he used to wrinkle his nose at and laughingly say, 'It's not fair.' At last year's *Big Weekend*, I introduced Cass to Yannis, Foals' lead singer, and explained the scenario. Yannis said he'd make it up to him and, later that day, he was true to his word. When they played 'Cassius' to a pocked crowd he told the story and dedicated the song to Cass, which has made being 'second best' that little bit easier to bear.

When Cass was born, my Mum was there, which was very precious. I just wanted to share the experience with her and for her to witness the birth of one of her grandchildren. It really was very special and a memory for all of us to cherish. He came out pretty damn quickly so there was no time for music at all, although the song I'd intended to have playing was David Gray's 'This Year's Love' so, in my head, that is very much Cass's song.

We were out of London by the time Cass was born, and this time the return to work wasn't so easy. We hired a nanny to work alongside Dad, because his arthritis means he can't do babies as easily as older children. Ria was amazing with Cass and the kids all love her – she still comes to the house and does art classes with them. But I had to go back to work when Cass was three months old and that meant not seeing him for the best part of ten hours a day. It was a real wrench – totally different from Jude; I'd seen him here and there throughout the day and kept breastfeeding him for quite a while. I struggled a lot with going back to work after Cass, and did wonder at times why we'd moved. I remember weeping a lot on the platform at Milton Keynes station. Steve was working really long hours back then and was often not home until after ten at night, by which time I'd be out cold, surrounded by the kids. Our only time alone together was on the morning commute down to London and it quickly turned into a bit of a farce; we'd bicker the whole way in. One morning Steve was on the platform without me, and a fellow commuter asked Steve why he wasn't with his wife. Steve explained that I wasn't coming in that day and the man told him: 'You two argue the whole way in, every day, right up until when you say goodbye to each other at Euston. Are you still together?' Steve found himself explaining that we do really love each other and have always got on really well, but that the morning commute was just our only opportunity to get through house business. He wasn't sure he'd convinced the man that everything was OK in our world. In any case, after that we decided to get separate trains, which cut down the conflict considerably.

When Jude was three years old he began to complain of tummy pains and to go off his food. He's never been a big eater but his stomach ache got stronger and stronger and he started to refuse all foods. Soon he was existing pretty much on a diet of milk and nothing else. Repeated trips to the doctors found nothing wrong. Time and time again we were told that it was probably just glands in his stomach, and that he'd grow out of it. This carried on for months and months, and the little blonde bundle of energy that we knew started fading in front of us. Each day I'd return home from the show to find Jude lying on the sofa with his beloved grandad stroking his tummy, hour after hour. Eventually he deteriorated so much that he was admitted to hospital for tests where the doctors continued to scratch their heads with furrowed brows and administer painkillers, which began a cycle. We'd go in with a sickly boy, he'd get painkillers, he'd miraculously rally round and would be pronounced better. We would be sent home no nearer to finding the root cause of his illness. At one point, the doctor did suspect appendicitis and Jude was prepared for surgery. I stayed with him and we were visited by the surgeon at about ten in the evening, who prodded him a bit, pursed his lips, sucked in some air and decided Jude didn't have appendicitis. He was given more painkillers and we were back to square one again.

A couple of weeks later, after many more hours of tender tummy rubbing from Grandad, Jude and I were back in hospital. By this point he was deathly pale and stick-thin, and we spent a long, restless night on the ward. A new doctor came on duty in the early hours of the morning. She took one look at Jude and declared that there patently was something very wrong with him and that no one could work out what it was, so he should be transferred immediately to Oxford. Thank God she made that judgement. We went straight by ambulance to the John Radcliffe hospital, sirens blaring the whole way. I remember looking at Jude and feeling white with fear that he might die. He looked as though life was draining from him, moment by moment. A specialist was called out from home – I remember him rushing into the room in his Saturday afternoon civvies – rolling up his sleeves and beginning to examine Jude's little body. He found a mass and, at that point, time froze. We were suspended in a capsule of unreality, Steve and I clinging to each other, trying to keep Jude awake for fear that if he closed his eyes and fell silent he might never speak again. After what felt like an eternity, the specialist turned to us and gave us the verdict. The dark mass was not, as we all feared, a tumour, but an abscess. Jude's appendix had burst and a large sac of pus had accumulated and had to be removed immediately. Jude was wheeled away into the operating theatre while Steve and I hugged each other in relief. Although Jude was facing potentially dangerous surgery, at least we knew what was wrong with him. He was in capable hands.

After saying goodbye to Jude – when your child has an anaesthetic they ask that you stay with them until they fall asleep and encourage you to say 'goodbye', which fills you with fear. Do they know something they're not telling you? Goodbye sounded rather foreboding, but we said our farewells and headed for the hospital canteen. I can remember eating peach crumble and custard with a large mug of tea, both of us giddy with relief. After the operation, which confirmed what the specialist had found, we all stayed in hospital for a while. Steve would sleep by Jude's side and I'd sleep in the parents' room, going to London each morning to do my show, and returning straight afterwards to give Steve a break. At no time during those days did I mention what was happening to Jude on the show. I don't know how or why I did that, but I just completely divorced the reality of my home life from the professional and focused on the minutiae of life on air. I think that, in some way, I was clinging on to normality – almost willing things to return to the way they'd been by maintaining the routine of my working life. I don't know whether I'd keep doing the show if one of the children became ill now. I'm less anxious about the job; I don't think I'd have the same feeling that it'd disappear if I missed a few weeks. But they'd been so good about my taking maternity leave twice in relatively quick succession that I didn't want to push my luck. I don't think it even crossed my mind that I couldn't be there. That's the thing about being a working mother – you might have all the systems in place, but no amount of planning and organisation (and, to be honest, I'm one of the least organised people I know) can help you through those times when your child is sick; they need you, and you're completely torn between your responsibility to them as their mother and your responsibility to your job, your employers, to the people (in my case) who tune in to listen to you each day. It's a tough call sometimes.

Coco Lux Francesca Whiley-Morton – 2008

Noel Gallagher is responsible for Coco. Now Steve was really happy with three children . . . but I've always known I wanted four. India, Jude, and Cass came along really quickly and without us thinking too much about it. Then the years flew by, and every now and then I'd ask Steve whether it wasn't time for number four. He'd come up with a million reasons why it wasn't right then, all of them quite sensible; to do with work and having three already, and life just getting back on a relatively even keel and Dad doing such a brilliant job as the manny. But if ever I closed my eyes and pictured the Whiley-Mortons, there was a phantom fourth child trailing along at the back. And, if I'm honest, that phantom fourth was a little girl.

Then I ran into Noel and his girlfriend Sara, shopping in Selfridges. I always seem to run into him shopping. I was a bit embarrassed, because the last contact I'd had with him involved me zooming along in the car, packed with the boys and India. I was yelling at them all because they were shouting so much; I was doing all those things we mothers do when we're alone and assume no one is listening – threatening to stop the car, remove toys, cancel play-dates. When we pulled over I saw that I had a missed call, from Noel. Somehow, while Cass was climbing around in the front seat, he'd managed to knock my phone and ring Noel, who then received a four-minute voicemail recording of the Whiley-Mortons on tour. Mortifying. In any case, I may have looked a little sheepish when I ran into him, but he was looking radiant. He and Sara had their new baby boy, Donovan, with them. Little Donovan was just a few weeks old, and Noel and Sara were so happy, and made it look so easy, cosy and fun, that I decided then and there that the day had come. (When I announced that I was pregnant I texted Noel and told him it was all his fault, and he said that in that case I should call the baby Noel, but I couldn't then blame him if it turned out to be trouble.)

So Steve and I had our day of reckoning. I pointed out to him that we couldn't really put off making the decision 'until next year', as we'd been doing for so long, because 'next year' I'd be forty-two, then forty-three, and so on. It's the greatest cause of anxiety for women, I think. We're all ageing so much more slowly; fifty is definitely the new forty. It amazes me that some of the great musicians I've known for the best part of twenty years – REM, U2, Madonna – are pushing fifty. Even dear old

Noel Gallagher has passed the forty mark. And yet women are still up against the great barrier of their fertility. I may be youthful, fit, slim(ish), into fashion, all the things that make it increasingly hard to judge whether a woman is thirty-five or forty-five. But, according to all the statistics, I'm reaching the end of my fertility, or the age at which it's considered safe to have children. But it's there for all of us, and it was looming ahead of me, and so I gently reminded Steve that it was now or never.

I think that what made it seem possible for us to have a fourth, particularly in Steve's mind, was his big career change. In all the years he worked for record companies, first for Virgin and then EMI, he worked incredibly long hours. Because we're out in the sticks, he'd often stay down in London if he had to see an act or entertain people. When the boys were tiny, we were in a bubble of the three kids and me a lot of the time. It was me who raced back from London to take over from Dad. Steve had always dreamed of managing bands and he was becoming increasingly exasperated by the corporate side of his job. It was a risk, but he decided to take it. So far, it's been a great success. But it's also had a huge and positive effect on our family life, because Steve's around so much more. He marshals the troops in the mornings until Dad pitches up, and is in and out in the afternoons while the kids are there. He's still working really hard, longer hours often, but he's much, much happier, and India and the boys have really benefited from this. (And now we have Coco, he's been really hands on with her, in a way he wasn't able to be with the other three.)

So Steve caved in, and we conceived Coco. I did a pregnancy test at home one afternoon and then flew into a panic. I really didn't want Mum and Dad to know until we were sure the baby was OK and so I decided I couldn't put the test in the rubbish or Dad might find it. Steve and I were going to the Brits that night and, at the last minute, I shoved the test in the pocket of a coat I wear when I'm walking the dog. As our car drove up to the red carpet my phone beeped and there was a text from India. 'Be careful what you drink tonight – you being with child 'n' all . . .' My blood ran cold. How did she know? I did the red carpet thing, my stomach churning, then called Indi and asked how she felt about being a sister again. 'What? So you really are pregnant?' India shrieked. It turned out that she'd put the coat on to walk the dog, shoved her hand in the pocket and found the test. But the line indicating a positive result had faded and so she didn't actually know that I was pregnant. I'd stitched myself up beautifully. It seems so odd that she put on a coat she'd never worn before that very night. It's as though her daughterly sixth sense led her to find it. Poor India had to keep my pregnancy a secret from the rest of the family until twelve long weeks were up. Steve, India and I had to go through the nightmare that I've been through four times now, and which to a certain extent all women go through – especially older women. I have to wait until about twelve weeks to be tested to see whether my baby is affected by *Cri du Chat*. I've always been quite clear in my head that I'd have a termination if my baby did have the condition. Frances is a wonderful person and a blessing to our family, but having lived through my childhood and seen what my parents went through bringing her up, I couldn't do that to my family – to Steve, to my children, to my mum and dad. They test for *Cri du Chat* using a form of amniocentesis, in which they take cells from the amniotic fluid and grow them in order to be able to look at the genetic make-up of the baby. As always seems to be the case with my life, I had a huge amount on, and I was getting rounder and rounder – having trouble fitting into my jeans, wearing baggy T-shirts, feeling nauseous. But I couldn't tell anyone that I was pregnant, not even Mum and Dad; I didn't want them to worry. So it was just Steve, India and me playing the waiting game. And, to cap it all off, I was due to fly to New York to interview Madonna, right about the time that I'd be twelve weeks pregnant.

It was such a surreal time; on the surface I was working away, on a glamorous trip to New York to interview the Queen of Pop, and all the time there was this other narrative going on in my head, and in conversations with Steve, about this unborn child and not knowing whether our future included her or not.

Meanwhile, the date I was to fly out was looming. We had the tests done at the Portland Hospital because it's just up the road from work. I kept calling them and asking whether they'd been able to make enough of a culture to look at the chromosomal makeup of the baby and they kept saying that I should call back the next day. This seemed to go on and on and in the end I couldn't even bear to phone, because I knew they'd either tell me it was fine, or ask me to come in, and then I'd know it wasn't OK. In the end I'd be at the studio doing my show and emailing Steve, saying, Have you heard? And then finally, the day before I was due to fly out, Steve rang and said, It's all fine, the baby is fine. The relief! I immediately asked Steve the sex. He laughed and said the doctor had told him they hadn't tested for the sex, because we'd seemed undecided as to whether we wanted to know. We're always so busy and stretched and we never see each other – or, at least, not alone – so there I was, lying on the table with my legs in the air, and when the doctor asked, 'Do you want to know the sex?' I answered 'No' and Steve answered 'Yes' – at the same time! The doctors couldn't believe we hadn't discussed this in advance. And a slight disagreement ensued. So we clearly appeared undecided to them, which was fair enough.

I got on the plane to go to New York the next day. I didn't want to announce to the world that I was pregnant until I'd told my family, and so I did my interview with one of the world's most toned, svelte women feeling decidedly round and squished into my clothes.

Children are so brutally honest. When I told the boys I was pregnant with Coco, I thought they'd be delighted at the idea of having me about the place a bit more, but Jude's first question was, 'But you're going back to work, aren't you?' I think he was worried that the days of the great perks – weekends at festivals, meeting his heroes the Mighty Boosh backstage at Wembley, premieres of all the latest movies – might end. Then, on the first day of my maternity leave, there was a near mutiny when I got them up and gave them breakfast: 'We want Grandad!' Apparently sitting round the table eating cereal and chatting with their mother didn't quite match up to my dad's breakfast routine of bacon butties on bean bags in front of the telly.

India was born by Caesarean, Jude and Cass were natural births and all went well. This time around, I think I'd decided that it'd be easy as pie. I went off air a couple of weeks before my due date and, of course, once I stopped, I realised how utterly knackered I was. My iron count kept falling and one minute I'd be zooming around the place buying buggies and ordering things online and doing all sorts of unnecessary jobs which suddenly seemed crucial, and the next I'd be flat on my back in bed, watching *Deal or No Deal*, unable to move, but surrounded by small boys and Nintendo games and India and her homework and the dog.

Coco ended up arriving ten days late. There was much discussion about whether she should be an elective Caesarean – they're always prepared to do that with older mothers and, in fact, I think my consultant would've preferred it. I kept swinging between thinking it'd just be simpler and feeling as though that wasn't what nature had intended. In the end, Steve got out a coin and said, 'Right, we'll toss on it. Heads, Caesarean, tails, natural.' But then I had a moment of total clarity and said that it'd be a natural birth. So Steve cleared his diary and we just waited, took walks in the woods with the dog and mooched about. Steve had only one thing; he just couldn't miss a gig on the Saturday in Brighton. That day I felt twinges, but I was sure they weren't really strong enough, just more Braxton Hicks. So I told him to head off, all was fine. I took the kids to see a film and then to eat out and, all the while, the contractions were gradually getting stronger but I didn't want to worry Steve, so I kept quiet. We watched the *X-factor* final, but it was while watching *Heroes* that I felt an almighty contraction and I said to India, 'Do you know, I think the baby's coming.' Indi was amazing. Totally calm and businesslike. 'We have to time the contractions,' she told me, and went and fetched a piece of paper and pen. When she'd ascertained that they were five minutes apart, she decided we needed to get to the hospital. So she rang my dad and our neighbour, who came over straightaway, took one look at me and said I'd better get going. Poor Steve was stuck down in Brighton with the band when he received a rather hysterical phone call telling him he needed not to bother coming home, but to meet us at the hospital. He made it back by about 1 a.m. and until then, India did all the work, holding my hand and talking to me. When Steve got there, he asked her if she wanted to go home and she said no, she didn't. And she stayed with me right through. We kept asking her if she wanted to go home or wait outside, but she didn't, and all I can remember is her there, eyes as big as dinner plates, leaving the room now and then, but totally involved.

She's doing an A-Level in photography. She took a series of pictures of me when I was about nine months pregnant – amazing, intense shots of me wearing a bra and knickers with very extreme make-up based on Courtney Love and things like 'EXIT' painted on my belly, with an arrow pointing downwards. India's instructions were that I was to look as though I were thinking, 'What have I done?' And I was thinking to myself, 'Well, that's not going to be too tricky, is it?' God knows what her photography teacher made of them. Parents' evening was interesting after she'd handed them in, I can tell you. And now her follow-up will be shots of her mother giving birth. We have an amazing shot she took of me, screaming my head off as Coco came out.

Steve was fantastic, of course. I'd started to get too tired; it was 4 a.m., which is a ridiculous time to be giving birth, and I reached the point when I was ready to give up, I really was. Steve took control, became quite bossy, and got me pushing with India offering very vocal encouragement from the side.

After Coco was born, Steve went home to get the boys up and Indi and I just lay there, in a sort of delirious fog, drifting in and out of sleep, watching Coco and saying, 'Look what we've done.' It was the most precious time. I'm so proud of her and so grateful to her for being there with me. Steve and I did worry that we'd traumatised her. For the first twenty-four hours or so she had that extraordinary look in her eyes women have after they've given birth: primal, intense. And she did announce that she was NEVER doing that herself. But now I think we have this wonderful thing that we went through together – she knew on the same day I did that I was pregnant and she was with me right through until the moment Coco was born. And if you think about it, it would've been entirely normal for her to be there not so very long ago – in generations past, all the women in a family helped out at a birth. And I think it really helped her because she's on the threshold of adulthood – she'll go away to college next year – and here was another little girl arriving to take her place. But now she has an intense bond with Coco that she'll never lose.

That first night we were back from the hospital, I ended up in bed with all the children, gradually one by one they passed out. We have this enormous bed now, to fit them all in. And there I was at one end, with Coco passed out next to me, then Jude, then Cass, and then India squeezed in at the other end, watching TV. I had an amazing moment of recognition – all these people were mine, Steve and I had made them. I took a photograph of them all, which I will treasure, just as I treasure that moment. We named her Coco Lux Francesca (for Frances). She's such a lovely little creature. And she's so like India, although she's darker, with Steve's dark hair (or the dark hair he had before he became a silver fox) and blue, blue eyes. She has a fantastic set of lungs on her, but she's dreamy and gorgeous and we all love her to bits. Now I know for certain that the Whiley-Morton tribe is complete and Steve is completely happy with four children.

Playlist – Coco's birth:

Here is the track list I prepared for Coco's birth. Everything was different having a baby sixteen years after my first, right down to the technology. My track list for India's birth was on a cassette, onto which I'd laboriously recorded the songs. With Coco, it was an iPod, naturally. This is what I was planning to listen to while I worked on producing Coco:

Elbow, 'One Day Like This' – such a brilliant, uplifting anthem.

Coldplay, 'Fix You' – makes me cry every time I hear it.

Elton John, 'Tiny Dancer' – the official anthem of Team Whiley-Morton.

Guillemots, 'Made Up Lovesong # 43' – just because it's such a beautiful song.

Burt Bacharach, 'This Guy's In Love With You' – more of 'our' music. Steve was a huge Burt Bacharach fan and turned me on to him when we first met. 'This Guy's In Love . . .' is a mostly instrumental track, with Burt crooning just a little here and then, like only Burt can. Steve and I listened to it all the time when we were first together and we still do. I remember having a 'moment' back in the day when I went to one of my first Oasis gigs and they played this song as an exit track when we were all leaving the auditorium and it was like a sign – they'd just played the most amazing set, and now they were playing our song. It took my love and respect for them as a band to a whole new level.

The Commodores, 'Three Times a Lady' – because I've loved that song since the seventies and it soothes me every time I hear it.

Glen Campbell, 'Wichita Lineman' – because I'm a cowgirl at heart.

Bob Marley, 'Three Little Birds' – Steve's really the Marley fan in our family, but this song's message – everything's going to be all right – is so fitting for childbirth, I think.

Adele, 'Make You Feel My Love' – her cover of a Dylan song, which really highlights the beauty and depth of her voice.

Kate Bush 'This Woman's Work' – all about a woman in the throes of giving birth from a man's perspective. So emotive.

I say that I was planning to listen to these tracks while labouring away. Things didn't quite pan out like that, though. When India and Barbara, our neighbour, were bundling me towards the car, I was busy insisting that I could drive myself. Somehow I'd managed to load everything I thought I'd need into my car. I fought them off, went to get in behind the wheel, and found myself bending double with an enormous contraction. The neighbour and Indi became very firm right then and more or less frogmarched me away from my car and my little overnight bag and my iPod! They were right to, of course, but at the time it seemed like a disaster. So Indi and I only had her iPod, which was new and didn't have much on it, to listen to at the hospital. Steve has an act called Cass Lowe, a singer-songwriter, and we had demos of five or so of his songs on her iPod, which we listened to over and over and which I'll forever associate with Coco. But she had some rather odd stuff on there, too, and I was working my way through a huge contraction when suddenly Elton John's 'Step Into Christmas' burst on, much louder than what we'd been listening to before. It was like being transported into hell and not even seasonal – Coco was born in October. I remember shouting 'Will you turn that fxxxing song off!' Then, shortly after Coco was born, the festive season hit and I'd be in a shop and that track would come on and I'd be transported back to the labour ward. A truly bizarre song to associate with childbirth.

The Little Noise Sessions have become incredibly important to me, and I know that they've done great things to raise the profile of Mencap. When I first told the people at Mencap that I was pregnant, and that the baby was due right at the time of that year's sessions, you could've heard a pin drop in the room – literally stunned silence before they pulled themselves together and congratulated me. I understood their horror. Initially I thought about handing over the reins to someone else for that year. But, in the end, I couldn't bring myself to do it. It's my baby and so nothing – not even the birth of my real baby – was going to stop me from organising it and from trying to be there for at least some of the sessions. The bulk of the organising (and favour pulling in) was done while I was still working. I'd hoped that Coco would be born a little early, so that I'd be in reasonable form for the gigs. But that wasn't to be.

I knew I *had* to be there for the first session, because I'd pulled in a huge favour and asked The Killers to make a surprise appearance. They turned up first and played four songs or so, including a fabulous cover of Cyndi Lauper's 'Girls Just Wanna Have Fun'. Brandon Flowers is the sweetest man, very shy and peculiar, with this eerie charm.

If we lived in London I could have fed Coco and dashed out to the gigs and then dashed back again. Instead, Steve and I had to come down from Milton Keynes, bringing Coco with us. So she was at her first gig at the age of two weeks old, and made her first stage appearance (during which she remained sound asleep) that night. I was still on a post-birth high, I think, and feeling invincible. Brandon is a father, too, and he loves children. Someone took a photo of him, me and Coco, for all the world looking like a lovely little family unit.

It's funny, because the first time I interviewed The Killers was years ago, when Brandon was probably only twenty or so, and they were really difficult to interview, silent and (I thought) hostile. I ended up directing all my questions to Ronnie, the drummer, because he was so much more open than the rest of them. I was thinking that they hated me and the interview. But when we were finished, I told them how much I loved their album, how brilliant I thought it was. And Brandon immediately relaxed and told me how nervous he'd been. He's incredibly shy, not an extrovert at all. He deals with this shyness by going out on stage in costume – that gold suit represents his public persona. I read once that he'd never go on stage in jeans and a T-shirt because then it'd be him on stage, rather than Brandon Flowers the rock star. So when I asked them at Glastonbury if they'd do Little Noise, I thought they'd say no. But they agreed to do it, and I knew just what a big deal it was for them to come out on stage in their jeans, as themselves, with the audience only a foot or so away. They were so nervous beforehand, and I was trying to reassure them, saying it'll be lovely, the crowd will be really up for it. And the crowd were, and it was.

After the high of that first night, I came down to earth with a huge crash. Razorlight were playing the next night, another huge favour for me as Johnny and Andy the drummer had appeared for me the year before. But I knew that I was just too exhausted to get down to London to do the introductions and so was poor Coco. So Steve rang Irwin, the singer from The Hoosiers. Irwin's a singer, not a presenter, and what's more he'd just sat down to a huge Sunday roast, cooked for him by his girlfriend.

But up he got and off he went, down to the Union Chapel and he did his bit for me, and I'm so grateful.

In the end, Coco and I only managed two other sessions. We were there for Damien Rice and Adele. Damien Rice has the reputation of being difficult to interview, but I've never had any trouble with him; he's a perfect gentleman, very clever and witty, and with such an extraordinary voice, which soared in the chapel. It was spine-tingling and India, Steve and I were transfixed and, fortunately, so was Coco. She remained peacefully asleep for the entire set – probably familiar with every song from her time *in utero*. Adele is a sweetheart, I've become really fond of her since we first visited her as part of the *Live Lounge* on tour. I turned up at her flat and there she was in her T-shirt and slippers, with a rotten cold, but just open and friendly and so, so funny. She sings a cover of a Dylan track, 'Make You Feel My Love', which I adore and she sang it for me on the night. I'd been planning to listen to it while I was giving birth to Coco, but events and Elton John got in the way. After that night everything fell apart, really. I got mastitis, from overdoing it, and trying to feed Coco backstage in awkward positions in five minutes flat. I was really very ill, she was hungry and distressed and we both did a lot of wailing. You live and learn – all that whizzing about and then endless phone calls and emails, when I should've been horizontal, lactating, snacking and napping.

Coco and I did manage to make it down for Keane. In my absence we were saved by some very special people.

Matt Horne from *Gavin and Stacey* was amazing; he introduced for me most of the nights that I couldn't be there, which was incredibly kind of him. And Edge from U2 came down one night. His niece Ciara has learning disabilities and works for Mencap and she asked him if he'd help out. He came along, although he's one of the shyest musicians on the planet, and introduced Kasabian, who were wide-eyed at the thought of being introduced by one of the members of U2. So many people did something to make those nights incredibly special. Needless to say, I'm hard at work getting this year's line-up sorted; I have some great tricks up my sleeve. Coco will be crawling around the stage by October.

I think, to a certain extent, Steve and I have maintained our sanity because our home and working lives are geographically separate. Steve works at home these days, but all his meetings and gigs are away from the home front, and so we get to pick and choose when we involve the children. But there have been times when my working life and my role as a mother have become entangled with disastrous, if hilarious, results.

One such occasion was the *NME* Awards last year. I was in the early stages of my pregnancy with Coco, but not yet telling people. I was stone-cold sober which, in hindsight, I realise was incredibly fortunate. India had become friendly with some of the cast of *Skins* and so she'd decided to come to the awards with me. Steve was at home with the boys – he's not overly enamoured of being at events as Mr Whiley, as he puts it. The entire cast of *Skins* decided that they'd tag along to the after-party with me and India. It was as though I'd taken a school trip to the awards – a school trip of exceedingly drunk teenagers. We weaved our way through the labyrinthine O^2 in Greenwich. I'd be at the bottom of an escalator making sure no one lagged too far behind, shouting at the ones at the top to wait. We made it to the party and then Indi and her mate Ollie proceeded to get even more wrecked. I was knackered, pregnant, in ridiculously high heels which were killing my feet, and aware of the fact that we had to get the train back to Milton Keynes that night. As the deadline approached, I started trying to round up India and her mate – just the one she'd brought along from Northhampton, not the cast of *Skins*. As far as I was concerned, they were on their own now. I dragged India and her friend towards the station, hurrying now, but having to turn and shout at them every five minutes or so. At one point I turned back to see the friend had lit up a cigarette. I was furious, because I know his mum and I felt I was responsible for him. I shouted at them and stormed towards the station, without looking back this time (the station is inside the O² complex, so I knew they were safe). When I did get to the station I turned back to shout again – and they weren't there. I phoned India and she said something completely incomprehensible, and then my phone went dead. I waited and waited and it got later and later. I was panicking by now. I had to keep going into a newsagent to buy something to get coins to call India on a payphone. She wasn't picking up. I called Steve, incredibly distraught, and told him I'd lost India in London. Various bands kept appearing to get the tube home, all pissed, and I'd borrow their phones to call her, but she still wasn't picking up. Finally, when I was ready to call the police, I rang Steve and he told me he'd spoken to India, she was at Euston and about to get a train to Milton Keynes. Somehow we'd missed each other and she'd gone straight down and on to a train without looking for me. Steve very sensibly told me to just get in a taxi and go to a hotel for the night, which I did. I'll never forget getting into a bath at 3 a.m., exhausted, my feet killing me, and looking down at my slightly swollen belly and feeling very lonely and sorry for myself.

The other side of the coin is trying to settle back into normal life after I've been away somewhere like Glastonbury. I live in a tiny village in the middle of nowhere and, while everyone knows what I do, they're by and large not that excited by it. There's a strange feeling, almost of loneliness, after you've been away on a jaunt – quite apart from the obvious joy and relief at seeing Steve and the kids. It's very strange chatting to the other mums in the playground and not feeling able to say, 'Yes, so I was out drinking with the Kaiser Chiefs until 4 a.m. the night before last.' (I'd sound like a complete tosser if I did announce that sort of thing.) It's yet another reason why Steve and I work so well together, because he knows my world. What I experience is a mini-version of what it must be like for bands to come off tour. I remember Bono telling me that his wife and children complain that he's very shouty for days when he gets back – his voice is pitched at 'Hello, Wembley!' level.

Most days I'm trying to juggle ten things at once, and buggering up every one of them. I feel as though I'm constantly spinning, like Dave Grohl, the whirling dervish. So many instances of cock-ups spring to mind when I think about it – knowing I was going to be away for work the week before Jude's birthday, so being super-organised and going to Toys R Us the night before I was due to leave, stocking up on presents, then leaving them in the car overnight with the doors unlocked. Very early the next morning, Steve and I heard Cass shouting, 'Jude! Jude! There's a remote-control K9 and a Necron Destroyer Lord in the car – come and see!'

As I've said, commuting down to London each day adds a layer of difficulty. I've made every kind of commuter error possible – I have to get a train from Milton Keynes to Euston and if I'm not concentrating at either end I end up on the slow train which stops a hundred or so times along the way, or, worse, end up on an express train to the wrong place – once it was Crewe. I've left most things on the train, too – never a child (yet), but my phone, changes of clothes, people's presents, the week's shopping.

If I'm around for a day or know I'm going to be back early in the afternoon, I try to organise play dates for the boys, since it's usually my dad who does all that – and loves it! Often I get back and there's a huge posse of children charging about, with Dad, generally dressed in a Kooks T-shirt, corralling them, handing out drinks and snacks, interceding in arguments. He says it takes him back to his days on the building sites.

I remember when the boys, started at a new school I felt that I had to be the one who organised some play dates; I was anxious about them finding new friends. So I cleared my diary for a week. Having rounded up a group of small boys, I got back to the house and found that I'd locked myself out. Steve wasn't there, Dad had the afternoon off. Somehow the horror of the situation (I felt as though a group of mums were watching from on high, frowning with disapproval), gave me superhuman strength and while the boys offered shouts of encouragement from below, I shimmied up a drainpipe and wedged myself through a tiny upstairs window. There was a terrible moment when I hung there, trapped like Winnie the Pooh, legs dangling in thin air, arms inside, flailing about above the loo. I still look up there now and wonder how I did it. Sorted, I thought, as I crashed to the bathroom floor. I then set about cooking tea for the boys. Halfway through his pork sausages the smallest boy looked up and said, 'Do you know that I'm a vegetarian?' I whisked the sausages away, handed him a sandwich, and spent the rest of the afternoon pondering whether to 'fess up to his mother. In the end I decided not to. Big mistake, of course – when she arrived to collect him he looked up at me, round-eyed, like a Midwich Cuckoo, and said, 'Are you going to tell my mummy what you did to me?' His name is Jake and he's now Jude's very best friend. Once I called him to arrange a play date only to be told by a strange voice that Jake had just gone on stage in Amsterdam. That'll be Jake from the Scissor Sisters then.

Another time I decided to be there to pick up Cass on his sixth birthday. Somehow I got carried away with the excitement. It ought to have been enough to be there at the gates, but at the studio that day I'd found a Spider-Man outfit which fitted me perfectly. The third film starring the man in blue and red had just been released, and Cass was a boy obsessed. I got into the outfit and Steve and I drove to the school. There's something liberating about being in costume. Steve sat in the car, laughing his head off at me, while I waited in the playground, getting into the spirit of things by pretending to climb the wall and practising my moves. A small crowd had gathered by the time Jude and Cass appeared and I was so absorbed in the role that I refused to speak to them, just continued to mime wall climbing and fighting evil-doers. The boys' friends thought it was fantastic, but slowly it dawned on me (and Steve, who was busy taking photos) that the boys weren't having such a great time. 'I know it's you, Mummy, because you've got such small boobs,' said Jude helpfully. 'Mummy, you're scaring me, please say it's you!' Cass squeaked. When I finally ripped off my mask, the boys made me promise, there and then, never to do that again. (I had to make do with wearing an elf outfit, face and head uncovered, at Jude's last party.) To this day, if I tell Cass I'm picking him up, he'll say, 'Not as Spider-Man, OK, Mummy? No funny business.' 'Please don't do it again.'

I think travelling brings out the worst, the very worst, in me. On our last big summer trip to Ibiza, we arrived at the gorgeous villa we were staying at late at night, and the guide took our luggage to the bedrooms. In the morning we went to unpack and couldn't find the children's suitcase. It was huge, and stuffed with enough clothes to last two weeks. I contacted the hotel reception, blamed them, then rang the airport and the airline and blamed them. I even had a go at Steve. Then someone said 'You did actually bring it with you, didn't you?' It was duly found at home on the bed where I'd packed it 24 hours earlier. I was massively relieved at not having lost everything, and hideously embarrassed at the fuss I'd made. The kids weren't thrilled as they had to spend the next fortnight in bad neon lycra shorts and *Ibiza!* T-shirts. I had to grovel to everyone. Consequently there's very little photographic evidence of them being on that holiday with us.

It's such a complex thing, motherhood, so all-consuming and defining, whether you work or not. Society dubs me a 'working mother', but that so often seems to be used almost as a term of abuse, as a way of indicating that women who work are distant mothers. I think I'm lucky in that I took to motherhood relatively easily. Nothing could have prepared me more for the chaos and ups and downs of caring for small children than having Frances for a sister. After watching my parents grapple with her (and continuing to do so), I know I've got it easy. Steve likes to say that, to some extent, I've recreated the patterns of life with Frances – the fact that she didn't sleep meant that nights Chez Whiley involved starting out in one bed, kipping there for a little, before moving to another. Nights Chez Whiley-Morton are pretty much the same. In my darker moments I wonder whether I'm a failure at disciplining the kids because of Frances; my default position is just to give in, or attempt to reason with them. But they're all pretty reasonable people, maybe as a result, and I think that, in the long run, treating them with respect and trying to see a situation from their point of view has paid off. I may get it wrong from time to time, and I certainly haven't spent every waking minute with them. Steve and I never stop thanking our lucky stars that Mum and Dad have been so hands on. (Since I've been back at work, Coco spends her days with Mum and Frances, while Dad handles the boys and India, when she needs it.) What it comes down to in the end is that we're a close, loving family unit, who operate as a tribe and are mostly pretty happy with one another and ourselves. Steve and I have four terrific children, and I believe that if we continue to look for the positive in each of them and encourage it, they'll make strong, confident adults.

Once again Andy and Ben were nothing less than 100 per cent supportive when I told them that I was pregnant again, that it was time for me to take stock and think about my future. And I'd half imagined that with Coco I'd decide that I'd had enough of work and want to be at home with her. I went back to work so early with the first three and with Cass, in particular, it was a terrible wrench. But my bosses at Radio 1 immediately said, 'When are you coming back?' The ratings for the show have been strong. I was surprised at how much this pleased me. And I also realised, pretty soon after Coco was born, that I really did want to go back to work. There's a feeling of guilt that I think all working mothers have, and no matter how much some people may insist that the world has changed, it is maternal guilt, not paternal. Nobody ever suggests a man is in some way cold or unnatural for wanting to work full time and have a successful career. But I love my job and my life, and I love my kids, and I think my working life gives me an energy and stimulus that I bring to being a mother. I just about make room for everything and everybody – even if most days I'm like a duck, sailing serenely over the water, while under the surface my feet are paddling furiously. It's important to me that my children – both boys and girls – will grow up with the idea that a woman can combine a successful, productive career with having children?

Playlist – the songs that always make me think about my four beautiful children:

Spice Girls, 'Wannabe' – I'll always associate the Spice Girls with India. I was working on *The Word* when they first appeared on the scene and I was naturally cynical about them as a manufactured pop band. But by the time India was five or six, she'd come to adore them and I saw them from the opposite side of the coin, as the parent of a fan. I took Indi along to the recording of an ITV Spice Girls special. I remember sitting in the audience with the likes of Richard & Judy and Jonathan Ross, all there as parents of children of roughly the same age. India was obsessed with Baby Spice and was dressed up with bunches in her hair, a leopard-print dress and bright-pink boots. We went backstage after the show was recorded and India got to meet her idols and they – and Emma Bunton in particular – were incredibly kind to her. We came away laden with Spice Girls paraphernalia. One of India's most treasured possessions for years was a photo of her with Baby and Scary. It was a great night, a perfect bit of mother–daughter bonding – I was very popular with my little girl for a long time after that night.

The Hoosiers, 'Worried About Ray' – they've become great friends of the Whiley-Morton clan, we've taken to going out on jaunts with them, wake-boarding and things like that. They're Jude's favourite band, and he's obsessed with Al, the drummer, who's become like a surrogate uncle. India, Jude and Cass are in the video for the track 'Cops and Robbers', set in London in the 1850s. Steve had arranged for Jude and Cass to appear as urchins. India tagged along for the ride and then found herself a role as a buxom barmaid, looking incredibly rough, with bruises and blacked-out teeth – not quite the Vixen she was hoping for.

Mika, 'Billy Brown' – we all love a bit of Mika, as I've said. He's like a member of the family and this is our favourite track – another car-ride special. The boys love the ambiguity of the words.

The Kooks, 'Naive' – we've all known the Kooks since Steve worked with them at Virgin. This track is another great family anthem, and reminds us all of a wonderful holiday we had on Ibiza, when we managed to take only two CDs, one of which was the Kooks, thankfully.

Ewan McGregor, 'Your Song' – India and I saw *Moulin Rouge* together and fell in love with this version of the great Elton John track. Another one that we like to sing at the top of our voices.

Pogues, 'Fairytale of New York' – the kids all love the Pogues and this song in particular, but I shuddered recently when we had it on in the car. The boys will sing along at the top of their voices, at the sweary bits they *really* sing along – enunciating every naughty word very loudly! No one asked me for an explanation, fortunately, so I just hoped that they hadn't really tuned in to the lyrics.

Almost Famous

In the looking-glass world of celebrity, I know where I stand. Like the title of the great film, I'm almost famous. People sometimes put the face to the voice that they hear on the radio, but I'm not an artist and I've never courted publicity. I occupy a sort of hinterland, a public figure to a small degree, but mostly just a civilian. There's a weird hierarchy that operates in the world of celebrity. I'm part of the machine, a cog in the wheel, but I'm not one of the chosen people, and I'm careful not to overstep the mark. You have to accept that the people you are interviewing can train an intense focus on you one day, and then not recognise you the next – it's something I've grown used to and I don't take it to heart.

It's such a personal thing, how you react to different people who've been important to you at some point in your life, when you finally get to meet them. I've interviewed so many famous names that I'm fairly blasé these days, but there are still people who render me starstruck. I've always been a huge fan of Rolf Harris – 'Two Little Boys' makes me cry every time I hear it. It's taken years for me to develop a style of interview where people feel they can open up to me. I'll already have covered what the release date of the LP is, or when the tour starts, what I want to know is the real stuff – what it's like to go on stage when you've got PMT or one of your kids is ill – and I've found that these are the questions that people want to answer because it's not just media waffle, but personal and relevant to them. I remember meeting him at Glastonbury with John Peel and being completely speechless, I just couldn't think of anything to say. I was transported back to being Johanne from Northampton, listening to him on the radio. But then I realised that Rolf Harris's mouth was hanging open: he was himself rendered dumbstruck by meeting John Peel, who had been a legend to him for years and years.

I've spoken elsewhere about there being a fame trajectory, which goes something like this: young, sweet and green at the outset, arsey, full of it and difficult when risen meteorically to stardom, wise and mellow once the early flare of fame has died down. Eminem provides a classic example of someone I've seen make this journey. When he first came in on the show, he'd just released 'My Name Is'. He was still a teenager; spotty, awkward, not terribly articulate. I felt really protective of him. When he next came in, around the time of the release of 'Stan', it was like interviewing a different person. By now he was a global superstar. He'd beefed up – and blinged up – considerably. He insisted on having the legendary Dr Dre with him, and they gave me such a hard time, competing with one another to see how often each could mention his (huge, of course) dick. The tables were well and truly turned – I was the vulnerable one, caught like a rabbit in the headlights, praying for it all to be over soon.

As I've said, I was totally unprepared for the level of attention I got when I began to do TV work, especially when I started hosting my own show. I accepted that people were going to be critical of my presenting style and the nature of the show – it'd be naive to do something so public, stick your head above the parapet, and then expect everyone to be nice to you. But what I hadn't expected was the level of attention – and vitriol – that was aimed at my appearance. At first I found it incredibly wounding. One lad's magazine likened me to a sci-fi character, Zelda, from the *Terrahawks*. Now I can laugh about that, because there's a resemblance of sorts but at the time it made me want to go about with a paper bag over my head.

There was a lot of detail about my weight, what I wore, the fact that I was often barefoot. The best piece of advice I received around this time was to weigh my coverage, rather than read it. I'm still very wary about press coverage and the internet, because you're always going to find something you don't like. There are certain writers on a couple of the tabloids who seem to delight in gunning for me every time I stick my head up and appear on TV. But as they say, you can choose your friends, but you can't choose your enemies.

We women may have taken several steps forward in terms of our right to work and to be open about having children, but things have taken a very bizarre turn with respect to our physical appearance. There's a whole culture obsessed with 'pap' shots of celebrities. These articles most often focus on weight – either dramatic weight loss or appalling weight gain. Suspected pregnancies based around an unflattering shot of a gently curved belly are very popular.

Like I say, I'm a civilian – I'm not a celebrity whose picture sells for thousands. But I'm still sufficiently in the public eye to sometimes be photographed in the street. There are often photographers outside Radio 1, particularly if a celebrity is coming in. When I was first back at work after having Coco I was photographed a few times with her in the buggy, which felt like a bit of an invasion of privacy. It always happens when I'm lugging coffees or a huge bag, or I'm looking particularly scuzzy and never when the hair's looking good and I'm wearing something OK. I've never quite figured out what to do about the paps. They're always incredibly familiar, yelling out your name and telling you how nice you're looking, and so it seems rude to ignore them. And some of them are just plain reckless; I'll cross a road and a pap will be running backwards in front of moving cars to get his shot, and I'll want to remind him that it's only me – I'm certainly not going to give him a shot that's worth getting run over for. When it first happened to me I'd panic and wonder what was going on – did a particular tabloid have a story on me? I'd find myself casting my mind back through recent misdeeds, usually involving my chosen vice, alcohol. It took a while for me to realise that they just do it on the off-chance that someone will want the shot – if there's something dreadful about your appearance, if your tummy is hanging out or your tights are laddered, *heat* might use it.

Last year I was photographed at the *Glamour* Women of the Year Awards. I was pregnant with Coco, and (with the help of Steve and Ellie my trusted stylist) I'd solved an enormous wardrobe crisis with a very beautiful floor-length blue dress. Unfortunately, it was raining very hard, and water soaked the hem and spread up the skirt, like rising damp. So, naturally, I was featured in a number of magazines in the 'fashion disasters' category.

I still struggle with premieres, although I'm well aware that it's a part of being privileged enough to be there. The paps really shout at you, yell your name so you'll turn in their direction, and the camera flashes are overwhelming. The kids have had to get used to it, because I can't take them to the premiere of a Harry Potter film without allowing them to be photographed. India is pretty resigned to it, although when she was first in her teens and far less confident about her appearance it was very traumatic. Jude, my performer in the making, is pretty relaxed about it, enjoys it even, and Cass hates it. But I always feel incredibly protective of them and hope that we haven't exposed them to too much, too young. And, as I've said, Steve is extremely good at disappearing into thin air the minute we hit the red carpet.

We've avoided the whole celebrity game by living outside of London and by being deliberately low-key. I can't imagine what it must be like for real celebrities who live in London and get photographed every day trying to go about their lives. It has to be especially difficult for people with children. I had a taste of it when Girls Aloud came to us for the *Live Lounge* tour. We had all the paps who'd followed them up from London hanging around at the front gate for the day.

I've struggled over the years not to let myself become obsessed with my appearance. Where do you draw the line? There comes a time when you have to make a series of decisions. The first, most important one, as Courtney Cox has said, is between your face and your arse: if you're too thin once you're past a certain point, you'll just look haggard. In order to be plump of cheek, you need to be a little plump of arse. Then there's always the lure of plumpers and fillers, peels and lifts. Personally I think do whatever makes you happy. For me it's going to the gym, cutting down on the drink, partying when my kids let me and getting a good night's sleep. Failing that, reaching for a pair of sunglasses and counting my blessings is a good fall-back. There's nothing like a big smile and inner glow to distract from the laughter lines. And, of course, I reserve the right to change my mind about all this as and when I feel the need!

I feel as though I have a responsibility to younger women, too. I guess I'm living proof that it's possible as a woman to gain admission to the boys' club that is the music industry. And more than that, it's possible to do so without having to 'be' anyone in particular, to use your sexuality or looks to get there, to pretend to be a boy or a very girly girl. And – most importantly – that you can do it and be a mother too.

When I began at Radio 1, there was just Annie Nightingale and me and a handful of producers. In putting together this book I've sifted through reams of photos and one thing that stands out, time and time again, is that the shots are so often of me standing with a band – name just about any band from the nineties – of men. There were exceptions, of course, but they tended to be placed in a genre of their own, 'girl bands', as though the fact that they were women was their unique selling point rather than the fact that Elastica, say, or L7, were making great music. Look at the music industry today – Duffy, Adele, Lily Allen, Amy Winehouse – all these great, intelligent, complex female acts that aren't just there because of their looks. When I was a teenager I hung around with boys far more than girls; it was the boys who were into music and were going to gigs. Now I look at India and her friends, and they're all really into music, boys and girls alike. I've been asked so many times over the years whether I saw myself as a role model and my answer has always been that I was just doing my thing and that gender didn't really come into it, but I know that's not quite true. And now I can see how much the world has changed, I think it's great if I'm counted as someone who made other women see what was possible. I look at Annie Mac now and she's so relaxed about who she is; not particularly girly, certainly not trying to be one of the lads. That strikes me as huge progress.

There have been times when I've really messed up. Thankfully, I've mostly managed to do it out of the public eye. Perhaps my most embarrassing moment was at Natalie Imbruglia's birthday party. For some reason, I was one of the first to arrive. The cocktails were flowing, I hadn't eaten anything that day, and I attacked them with gusto. I remember hitting the dance floor – always a really, really bad sign with me, as I'm not a dancer. If I'm out on the floor, I'm really pissed. I whirled around, having the time of my life, and then suddenly I knew I was going to be sick. I raced for the loo, made it, and was then violently ill. At some point I sobered up sufficiently to realise that the kind soul holding back my hair from my face and stroking my back as I leaned over the bowl wasn't Steve, but Natalie Imbruglia. It was late by then, and a queue of people, headed by David Walliams, had formed at the door, wanting to say goodbye to Natalie. She didn't leave my side, just managed to shout goodbye as we braced ourselves for the next bout. Poor Steve was outside the loos, engaged in a fierce row with the attendant, who was refusing to let him in to rescue me. He didn't realise I was being tended to by Natalie and thought I was slumped alone in a cubicle. Eventually he managed to get in to me. My next memory is of being carried by Steve out through the kitchens, managing to wave at amused chefs as I passed. We avoided the press out the front. We were staying in London, and Steve lugged me through the kitchen of the St Martin's Hotel, again so I wouldn't be spotted. I got many texts the next morning, including one from David Walliams which read 'Naughty, naughty'. That pretty much sums up my performance on that occasion – the single most embarrassing night of my life. And I'm not revealing a dark secret in these pages, either, because Scott Mills sweetly told the whole story on air . . .

There is also the slippery nipple incident. We were down in Brighton at a Radio 1 event and we were drinking cocktails again. I just don't learn. I was with James King, who did the film reviews on the show, and my producer of the time, Piers (who started out as tea boy on the Zoe Ball breakfast show, is now boss of the Chris Moyles breakfast show, can eat ten Krispy Kreme donuts in one sitting and was wearing pink long before the term 'metrosexual' was invented.) Anyhow, those two were entirely responsible for what happened next. I was given a Slippery Nipple, which is just Baileys and Sambuca, set alight. The idea is to get it down your throat very quickly, all in one go. I forced myself to swallow down the lot, and then felt it coming straight back up again. I ran for the loo, eyes watering, reached a revolving door at the end of the bar and in my blind panic couldn't get through it. As a mass gathering of my colleagues and various bands watched on, I spewed Slippery Nipple everywhere.

My worst moment in the public eye didn't involve booze, though. I'd had The Fray on the show and they'd jokingly said they wanted me to get up on stage with them. I'd said that the only thing I was good for was playing the tambourine and so they'd said OK, they'd get me doing a little percussion for them when they played at the Radio 1 *Big Weekend*. I thought (prayed) that they'd forget about it but they hadn't – they made it clear they fully expected me up there with them. *The Big Weekend* is a huge deal these days and the bands play to a capacity crowd in a massive marquee. I'd imagined tapping away at the back of the stage, but that wasn't what the band had in mind. I have no rhythm, no musical talent, and they were adamant that I was to be right at the front of the stage. So I swallowed my pride and launched in, banging away enthusiastically, not knowing where to look. I was dying inside. Then suddenly The Fray frontman Isaac Slade stopped the song, turned to me and said, for the whole crowd to hear, 'No, no, you don't come in yet – don't play until I tell you.' Oh the agony. I remain rooted to the spot after that, waiting for him to give me the nod. It was possibly the longest three or four minutes of my life.

As I've said, I really took a long time to get to grips with the world of fashion and, even now, I'm never happier than in a pair of jeans and some trainers or boots. Fairly early on in my career, I was introduced to Matthew Williamson at a party and summoned up the courage to tell him that I loved his clothes. He was super-friendly and warm and so down-to-earth that I knew we'd hit it off. He told me to come down to the shop and spent ages showing me what he thought I should wear, what suited my colouring and figure. Shortly afterwards Steve and I were invited to his fashion show and party afterwards. I agonised over what to wear. Steve kept saying he was sure I should be in a Matthew Williamson dress, but I had another one I was completely besotted with that I thought was really flattering. I insisted I should wear that, but I did, as a precaution, bring along one of Matthew's dresses. We pulled up in the car and got out and posed for photographers and went inside. The room was filled with beautiful women – Sienna Miller, Yasmin Le Bon, Keira Knightley – all dressed in Matthew Williamson. Suddenly it dawned on me that I was the only one not dressed in one of his outfits. Steve had been right! This is, I now know, the rule in the world of fashion, which is why you'll see everyone in the front row at a Chanel show dressed solely in Chanel. 'OK,' I hissed to Steve, 'we have to do that again.' So we snuck out the back, with Steve muttering, 'I told you . . .' I got back into the car and wriggled into the Williamson dress and then we drove up again, got out, all bright smiles, and were photographed once more. Thank God I'd brought the dress with me.

On another occasion I was presenting an award at the Brits. I'd bought a pair of shoes to wear, Prada, with a towering platinum heel. I thought they were the most beautiful things I'd ever seen. But they were solid metal and had no flexibility at all, and they were very high. They might've been used as an instrument of torture. I stood at the top of a steep walkway down to the stage and knew, without a doubt, that I'd fall flat on my face if I tried to get down there in those shoes. I had minutes to spare. There was nothing for it: I took them off and did the whole thing barefoot. I think it was assumed I was making a statement, particularly as I'd often presented my Channel 4 show barefoot, but it was merely a case of self-preservation. They were the most expensive shoes I never wore.

I have a fabulous stylist I use these days and life is so much easier. Ellie knows just what I like and she's very clever. My pre-stylist days were dark and filled with errors. I'd always leave the whole thing until the last minute and then race into a shop and grab the first thing that seemed vaguely appropriate and fitted OK. I remember on one occasion I was presenting the Mercury Awards for TV, did my usual last-minute trawl and came up with something neon green and T-shirt-like. Steve turned up at the show, recoiled, and said involuntarily (he's usually pretty careful about what he says to me because he knows how sensitive I can be), 'Christ, what are you wearing?' By then it was too late, I'd already filmed some links, and so I had to go through the rest of the night in that flash of neon, knowing that I'd made a terrible, terrible mistake. Sure enough the hideousness of my top was written about in the tabloids in the days that followed. Thank God *heat* magazine didn't exist back then.

To the extent that I have a public profile, I've tried to put it to good use. I'm really proud of my work for Mencap and it makes sense for me to use my name and my connections to help the charity, because of Frances. I'm also involved because I want to stop young people being prejudiced against people with learning difficulties – to stop young people pillorying them – to encourage acceptance. We all need to be drawn to helping a particular charity or group of people in need because of our first-hand experiences. I know at first hand what it's like to bring up a child with severe learning disabilities, and how ordinary people struggle with the amount of care that is available. I know the emotional side of the stresses placed on a family – things that can't be quantified financially but are as important. The amazing thing about Mencap is that it places an emphasis on providing social activities to help improve the quality of life of people with learning disabilities, and their families, rather than simply focusing on more obvious, financial needs.

In 2008, I went to Ethiopia for Comic Relief. Nothing could have prepared me for the things I saw when I was there. Before I went, I spoke to as many people as I could who'd gone to Africa. I remember Bono telling me, 'It'll change your life – you'll never be the same again.' He told me that his wife had asked him once why he didn't speak about his experiences in Africa, but, as he said, how do you put into words, even to the person closest to you, what it feels like to watch a child die? It was very comforting to be able to talk to other people who've been out to Africa when I came back, because I think that, unless you've been there and seen it, it's very hard to comprehend what it's like to be confronted with the fragility of human life.

I was there for the briefest time – five days – but it really was life-changing. I was on a trip with David Walliams and Matt Lucas, Ross Kemp and Rebekah Wade. We visited three special projects funded by Comic Relief, GOAL, St Matthew's, and The Integrated Holistic Approach to Urban Development. Not only do they run shelters for the one hundred thousand vulnerable street children in Ethiopia's capital, Addis Ababa, they also try to re-house and educate the poorest people living in slums outside the city. I remember finding it hard even to phone home, I was so intensely involved in what I was seeing. I spoke to Jude one evening and he started going on about a Lego toy Steve had brought him, and saying he wanted to get another one on Saturday. All I could think was that he didn't know how lucky he was – it was hard not to feel really angry with him, then I was furious with myself for giving my kids so many privileges. When I got back, I found myself constantly telling the children, 'I've just been to Africa, where the children have nothing.' I think it's really important that they know how fortunate they are. And they do, they're not entirely blind to it, because we've tried to educate them. Before I left to go on the trip, Jude came to me with his piggy bank and emptied it out, saying, 'Please give this money to the children in Africa.'

Something all of us on that trip struggled with was the desire to just hand out as much money as we could to everyone we met. The Comic Relief people were very firm with us, reminding us that if the money went to a charity instead, it would be put to use in such a way that as many people as possible would benefit. I completely saw the logic of this, and yet, at the same time, it was so hard not to give something to the little boy who thrust his hand through the window of our car.

Travelling with David and Matt was wonderful. We'd be in the most desperate situation, meeting people with AIDS on the brink of death, sick children, and the extraordinary people who cared for them, and I'd be close to tears, feel as though I was falling through the floor, and then David would say something inappropriate and hilarious and make it all possible to bear. It was because of his experiences in Ethiopia that David went on to swim The Channel for charity. I don't think anyone foresaw that.

He has hidden depths, does Mr Walliams, and is much to be admired. Although when it comes to humour he's a deeply sick individual.

One day we visited a refuge for girls who'd been raped, often while they were still very young. They each got up and told their story and then they sang beautifully for us. I sat there with tears pouring down my face, feeling utterly helpless. Then Matt got up and said that we must sing for them and so he began to sing 'King of the Road' in his rich, deep voice, and we all joined in. It was a great moment because it felt as though we were thanking them for their performance in a fitting way.

I remember going to one particular project and being anxious about what I'd see, but as we arrived there was just this explosion of clapping and singing. These were people riddled with disease, starving, dressed in rags, and yet I sensed an incredible serenity in them, which I found really humbling. We're all so ridiculously privileged in the West, and yet so much time and energy seems to be spent worrying about whether we're happy. But I'm aware that it would be ridiculous to romanticise the way people in Africa live. I saw children as young as seven, orphaned, begging and living on the street, and countless people who'd lost eyes and limbs in the civil war. We went to a night shelter and I met girls of twelve or thirteen – about the age that India was then – who'd turned to prostitution to survive. India will never have to do that, and yet the only difference between her and them is the accident of birth.

I got to the airport to fly home and realised I'd left my plane ticket in my hotel room. Someone had to drive back and get it for me – not entirely out of character, but pretty chaotic even for me. I think I was in a sort of dream, absorbing everything I'd seen and done. When I realised my mistake I broke down in tears, and the floodgates opened. I just couldn't stop crying. I wasn't really crying about my ticket (although it sat particularly badly that a worker had to waste valuable time and fuel making good my mistake), but for all the people who'd met over the past few days

– like a sort of catharsis. I cried and cried. I don't think Matt and David knew what to do with me!

The most troubling moment for me was meeting a woman who had lost her husband to AIDS, and was infected herself. She had this beautiful baby boy, just over one, and she was crying to me, saying, 'Who'll look after my baby when I'm gone?' I came away feeling a sense of responsibility to that woman and her boy. We broadcast my 'African Diary' on the show over the course of a week in the build up to Red Nose Day and the response was wonderful. What I came to see after that trip is that all of us in the over-privileged West have a responsibility to the whole, messed-up, struggling continent – Africa is *our* problem. This year, a brave Comic Relief crew, skippered by Gary Barlow, and among them Radio 1's very own Chris Moyles and Fearne Cotton, climbed Mount Kilimanjaro and raised a huge sum of money. It was a gruelling trip for them all, and an amazing feat.

Music Junkie

As soon as I'm asked – as I often am – to list my favourite bands or the bands that have most influenced me, I realise how diverse my musical tastes are. I was an indie girl for years, from those Brighton days of goth music and even before then, when I loved The Clash and New Order and Cabaret Voltaire. But if I cast my mind even further back, there are the great days of disco, Bee Gees, ABBA, soul tracks like Jocelyn Brown's 'Somebody Else's Guy' and Chaka Khan's 'Ain't Nobody', all those hours spent on the dance floor. Later, like a thunderbolt, there was the whole early nineties dance scene and the excitement that went with it. So, I'm hard to pin down, but I think that the single aspect of a band or act that I'm drawn to, time and again, is the voice. One of my all-time favourite tracks, as you'll see later, is 'Ol' Man River' sung by Paul Robeson, from the musical *Show Boat*. It's the richness of his voice I adore.

I loved Björk from the days when I first heard The Sugarcubes and the song 'Birthday'. I remember finding the raw, discordant quality of her voice extraordinary. They came in to do WPFM and after the show we went around the corner to the pub. I was transfixed by Björk – she was elfin and magical. Later that night we saw their gig at The Town and Country Club in Kentish Town and I was amazed by their wild energy.

I remember hearing Sinead O'Connor's song 'Troy' – with that eerie quality to her voice, as if she's both singing and speaking the lyrics. It's an operatic quality in those two women vocalists that I responded to. I often react to what you might call a fragility; certainly an ability to convey emotion. Because of that, I'm not always drawn to the best singers. The leads in some of the bands I've liked most in the last few years aren't always note-perfect, but they sing with all their soul. Lyrics get me too – the poetry in a song is far more important to me than the simple, raw energy of an indie guitar track, which though it might have a great hook to it often leaves me cold. I'm a huge fan of My Chemical Romance, for example, because of that unique quality to Gerard Way's voice. And I love Damien Rice as much for the power of his words as for his extraordinary voice. One band I haven't spoken about elsewhere is The Cure. I was a huge fan way back and again it's because of Robert Smith's voice, raw with emotion, childlike and true. He was this fascinating creature, otherworldly. He sings songs that tell a story, that take you into a world – in the way that the Stones do, even in the way that Eminem's 'Stan' does. My favourite garment is a Cure T-shirt. Not just any T-shirt, mind. I bought it when I was doing *The Jo Whiley Show* and it cost £700 more than a decade ago. I think I split the cost with the show. It's been money well spent, because I'm still wearing it and one day I'll have it framed. It's a work of art – Robert Smith's face and the name of the band, etched in chunky diamantés. The Cure saw their videos and music as equally important and the two together as an art form. I think they may have influenced Green Day, who also understand how to transform live performance into an audio-visual spectacular.

Don't know about you but I love a list – here are some of my vital statistics – the acts and tracks that are most important to me, and why.

Playlist – greatest musical influences:

The Platters – My Dad was crazy about this 1950s African-American *a cappella* group. I must've heard 'Smoke Gets In Your

Eyes' a million times when I was growing up, and their four-part crooning harmonies instilled in me a love of vocals. It's no surprise that I love Fleet Foxes, for the same reason. I like music in which the voice takes precedence as opposed to the guitar – my idea of hell is Pink Floyd and all that prog rock. It was the days of those huge cartridges, which Dad would clunk into the machine in the car, so huge it seemed as though there wouldn't be room for anything else, and then off we'd go, the Whileys on tour, soothed by those rich voices.

Barry White – The Walrus of Love himself. Barry takes me back to those days of disco, with his sexy, throaty voice. I used to imagine an incredibly smooth, sexy guy, and was truly surprised when I first saw a picture of him. But his voice was unique, and he wrote the most beautiful, heartfelt love songs. My favourite was always 'Never, Never Gonna Give You Up'.

New Order – They went on to become incredibly important to Steve and me, but my love of New Order stretches back into my teenage years. As with most of the music I was into back then, I associate them with wanting to become part of the coolest crowd at school. I was invited along to a sixth form party, which was unusual and I was really chuffed about it. There was a boy there with a tape with Depeche Mode and New Order on it. I remember 'Blue Monday' coming on and stopping in my tracks and listening. It seemed so new and different and exciting: the pulsing rhythm, the fragile sound of Bernard Sumner's voice. Everything about them was groundbreaking – they were true dance music pioneers. Over the years I've tried to clear away my vinyl and CDs, hone them down, but there are some things I'll never throw away, and my New Order records are one. It's not just that I loved them so much; it's also the fact that Peter Saville's album covers are works of art in themselves.

The Commodores – on any laid-back playlist I create, hangover playlists or Sunday morning playlists, there's always a Lionel Ritchie or Commodores song – 'Easy' or 'Sail On'. But my very favourite, the one that transports me back beneath the silver ball at the swimming club disco, still wondering if he'll ask me to dance, is 'Three Times a Lady'. Inevitably, he never did.

The Bee Gees – I have a vivid memory of standing rooted to the spot in my Grandma's front room, staring at the TV screen as the brothers stalked through a town in Italy, each clad in an agonisingly tight-fitting pair of white flares as they sang 'Tragedy'. One of the few times Dad put his foot down was when he refused to let me see *Saturday Night Fever*, but I had the gate-fold album and I loved every track. Through that I worked my way back and discovered their early material – such extraordinary vocal harmonies. My favourite is 'New York Mining Disaster'. They're responsible for some superb tracks sung by other artists, too – 'Guilty' by Barbara Streisand and 'Islands in the Stream', the version sung by Kenny and Dolly, is magnificent. They represent British song-writing at its finest.

The Clash – I was late discovering The Clash, after that seminal gig in Birmingham, but I got to know and love *Combat Rock* first of all – especially the tracks 'Should I Stay or Should I Go' and 'Rock the Casbah' – I remember them performing it on *TOTP* and loving every second of it. Then I worked my way backwards through their earlier albums. I think my all-time favourite track is still 'White Riot' because I was lifted up into the crowd for the very first time.

Guilty Pleasures:

My guiltiest musical secret is that I'm a sucker for musical theatre. I love *Show Boat*, *Cabaret*, and any film of a musical. And I've seen an awful lot of the stage shows, too. One of my great heroes is Baz Luhrmann, because he understands how to make the visual and the musical blend together to create a unified art form. My favourite films of his *Romeo & Juliet* and *Moulin Rouge*. I had him on the show and was bowled over by his charisma and charm – very unusual in someone who prefers life behind the camera rather than in the spotlight.

Playlist – other tracks I love but know I shouldn't:

John Denver, 'Annie's Song' – The words are so utterly romantic and beautiful, all about someone becoming everything to you – about falling in love. I remember Steve and I having a 'moment', when we'd just met and he confessed to loving that song and I was able to say 'Me too!'

Kelly Clarkson, 'Since You've Been Gone' – I was blissfully unaware of this track until I went on a karaoke night with my team and someone got up and belted this out and I've been hooked ever since. I think you'd find a lot of people screech this one out alone in the car. I certainly do. She's sung it in the Live Lounge since.

ELO, 'Wild West Hero' – ELO doing cod Cowboy and Indian music, but with plenty of their stock in trade synth violins thrown in.

Dolly Parton, 'Nine to Five' – I love this track and in fact I'm not even sure it's a guilty pleasure because Dolly is so great. 'I Will Always Love You' makes me cry every time I hear it – Dolly's version, not Whitney's.

Bill Medley and Jennifer Warne, 'I Had the Time of My Life' – from *Dirty Dancing*. Remember that film? Because I was busy being a goth or otherwise resolutely alternative, there's a whole era of films which I didn't see – *The Karate Kid*, *Top Gun* and *Dirty Dancing*, each with a soundtrack to go with it. Recently India and I decided to get educated and sat down to watch *Dirty Dancing*. We loved it; Patrick Swayze's toe-curlingly pert manoeuvres, Jennifer Grey's slightly hangdog pout, and that line I'd heard other people repeat so often – 'Nobody puts Baby in a corner.' When James King, who did the film reviews on my show left, I played 'I Had the Time of My Life' at the end of his last show and found myself welling up with tears.

First gigs:

The Rubettes – When I was nine or ten, Dad took a friend and me to see The Rubettes, that incredibly cheesy white-suited band, born out of the ashes of the glam rock era. I had a new outfit for the occasion, bought from Tammy Girl, and a crew-cut, courtesy of my ever-practical Mum. I thought I looked great. They played at a local sports arena, and because my auntie worked for the council, Dad and I blagged our way backstage, met the band and I had my picture taken with them. A seminal moment for us both; especially when I think how often Dad and I have been backstage together at gigs since.

Wham!, 1983 – The 1980s incarnation of George Michael, back when he was straight, teamed up with Andrew Ridgeley, shuttle-cock down his tiny little shorts, headband on, hair streaked and blow-waved. I wasn't a huge fan, but my friend Noel dragged me along and we came down to London to the Lyceum, which was terribly exciting. I loved the lyrics of 'Young Guns'; it's still a great track, for all that they were a little bit cheesy, and so is 'Club Tropicana'. We had a wonderful time, and George Michael's voice was – and still is – extraordinary.

Depeche Mode, 1982 – It was pretty forward of Campion School when I look back, but an impossibly cool group of upper-sixth formers occasionally organised school trips to see bands and that time I was asked by one of them if I'd like to join in. All of my early musical experiences involved boys – usually older than me – because my peers, the girls especially, weren't into music and that was all I really cared about. No teachers were involved and we headed off for the night in a school bus. I was a fan of Depeche Mode, but it was an incredibly low-key live performance; it was long before things got quite edgy for the band. Back then it was all very new wave; a group of coiffed young men tootling away on their synthesizers, Dave Gahan occasionally swivelling his hips. I had the greatest time though, hanging out on the bus. It was a world away from our usual school outings – ice-skating in Birmingham at Silver Blades.

Haircut 100, 1982 – So cheesy, but I loved them at the time and I must've listened to their album, *Pelican West*, hundreds of times.

Cabaret Voltaire, 1983 – A much more alternative band, whose sound was a blend of dance music and experimental electronica. I remember gaining brownie points early on by being able to tell the king of the alternative, Steve Lamacq, that I'd seen them play live back in the day.

David Bowie, 1982 – It was the *Serious Moonlight* tour, which coincided with the release of the *Let's Dance* album. People said he'd sold out and become commercial with this tour, but I loved it. It was pure theatre, such a spectacle – I remember the highly staged nature of the set, Bowie having an 'Alas, poor Yorick' moment with a skull, the huge globes being spun out into the audience and passed through the crowds, the endless costume changes. It was a precursor to the massive, high-production tours that everyone, from U2 to Madonna, has embarked upon since. My long-suffering Dad drove me and a friend, Stuart, to the Milton Keynes Bowl to see the gig, waited and then drove us back. We were nearly home, tired but happy, when my friend remembered he'd lost his wallet and Dad, uncomplaining as always, had to turn round and head back.

The Clash, 1982 – This was a defining moment for me, when I experienced the excitement and pure joy of seeing a band live. I'd been hanging out with a bunch of sixth form boys – I was always a bit of a tomboy. We'd gone waterskiing for the day, and they were going off to see The Clash that evening. At the last minute one of them said casually, 'Oh would you like to come along?' I was terribly pleased to be asked, although I knew nothing at all about The Clash, other than having seen them once on *TOTP*. It was May, early summer, and a warm day and I was wearing these little tiny canvas pumps, totally wrong for seeing a band live. But my friends made their way down the front and I followed them because they were all blokes. There we were, leaping up and down, and at one point I was lifted up into the crowd as the band played 'White Riot'. I was lost in the music and I remember having this feeling – 'Ah, so this is what it's all about.' It was my epiphany. By the time we left the gig late that night my shoes had disappeared and my feet were bloodied and trampled, but I was ecstatic. That was my introduction to live music. It couldn't have been better. It was like a homecoming.

Greatest live moments:

Foo Fighters, 'Everlong', Reading Festival, 1995 – As I've described elsewhere, Foo Fighters played at Reading in their early days and I managed to squeeze into the tent and knew I'd witnessed the beginning of something huge.

Coldplay, Glastonbury, 2002 – I've described elsewhere how much I loved seeing Coldplay up there, headlining at Glastonbury; just a few short years before that night Dad I had watched them play to a tiny crowd in a pub in Northampton.

Green Day, Milton Keynes Bowl, 2005 – Green Day are one of the great contemporary live acts. This gig was on a blistering hot day and they pulled every trick in the book – culminating in blasting the audience with red and white confetti just ahead of playing 'Good Riddance'. It was a perfect gig. They've come a long way from an angry young punk band; they are a huge stadium act these days and yet they manage the spectacle of a huge outdoor concert while still creating a sense of intimacy.

Muse, Wembley, 2007 – The spectacle that is a Muse concert equates in my mind somehow with a Baz Luhrmann film. The set was extraordinary, with massive screens behind them and a futuristic stage set. They had acrobats suspended from huge white balloons soaring above the crowd during a dreamy rendition of their song 'Blackout'. It was spellbinding and as they played hit after hit it was like looking back over my years at Radio 1. I thought back to those days of the *Evening Session* when they'd come in, the most unlikely looking rock stars I thought I'd ever met, and yet with such a big sound and a huge vision.

Arctic Monkeys, Brixton Academy, 2006 – This was a *NME* tour. I'd seen one of the Monkeys' very first gigs and now here they were before a big crowd at a famous venue. I was down the front among the band's adoring fans. The other bands on the tour joined them on the stage – We Are Scientists, Maximo Park and Mystery Jets – they'd obviously all bonded on the tour and it was genuinely moving seeing them embrace at the end of the gig. They played 'Mardy Bum', a track I just love – it was a tremendously euphoric moment.

Tracks I'd be happy never to hear again:

The Tamperer featuring Maya, 'Can You Feel It' – One of those terribly cheesy dance tracks that became huge and I had to play over and over, while inwardly smashing my head against my desk. At least I can turn down the music and take off my headphones when a track like that is playing.

Black Box, 'Ride On Time' – The act I failed to book on to *The Word*, and then 'Ride On Time' became a dance classic. I was so into grunge back then and I just couldn't see how they'd fit in with what we were doing on the programme. It might've been an error on my part, but I couldn't bear the song back then and I can't now – she screeches rather than sings.

I don't think I'm unusual in citing a really broad range of musical interests; I think that's very much the way things are heading in the world of music. I see it with India and her friends. I'd say that she veers towards indie music, but they embrace everything. When I was growing up there were tribes – I went through my goth phase, for example. And when Steve Lamacq and I were presenting the *Evening Session* it was still very much the time of the supremacy of *NME*. It was their role to find trends and give them a moniker – the new wave of new wave. But that's all over now. People look increasingly to the internet to discover and share their music. Bands can be launched and build up a huge fan base before securing a record deal; Mika, Adele, Florence and the Machine, all released their music on the internet and built up a following before the record companies got involved. It's an ever–changing landscape which has thrown the music business into a state of chaos. Furthermore things are changing at such a pace it's impossible to predict six months down the line let alone an eventual outcome.

Musical worlds have collided over the past couple of years and consumers and musicians are far more open to all kinds of music. That's why we get all kinds of weird and wonderful things going on in the *Live Lounge* from 30 Seconds to Mars covering Kanye West to Biffy Clyro covering Rihanna's 'Umbrella' – people are loving a much broader range of music and being far less cynical than a few years ago. Coldplay will be supported by Jay Z and Girls Aloud this year which just about sums it up.

The world has changed so much in the twenty years or so that

I've worked in the music industry. I think back to that day when Steve Lamacq and I were given a first pressing of the Oasis single 'Columbia'. Vinyl is now a thing of the past and the CD's days are numbered, hence the collapse of so many music retailers. It's all about downloading these days and that's having a huge effect on the way people listen to music. The music industry is in turmoil. Suddenly the power is leeching away from the record labels, because people can get hold of tracks they want to hear without buying an album – there's a far greater opportunity to hear stuff before you buy. Because of this live performances are taking on greater significance which, in part, I think explains the success of the *Live Lounge*. Recording studios are disappearing because the technology is so much more readily available. Even the concept of the album is under threat, as Bono said recently in an interview, because people are now downloading the tracks they like for their playlists, rather than listening carefully to a whole album, as we used to do. (Although we've all been putting together compilation tapes, the precursor to the playlist, for years.) Who knows where it will all end up, but I suppose the main thing is that people are still listening to music and there's still a huge appetite for new material and acts. Ultimately, everything has changed and nothing has changed: it's still all about a great song that speaks to the generation listening to it, and an image to go with that sound, which people can identify with.

Finally, my ultimate track list, which has taken a great deal of time and effort and agonising decision-making:

Elton John, 'Tiny Dancer' – The Elton I knew before I met Steve was the man who sang 'I'm Still Standing' on *TOTP*. I remember Steve explaining to me how important it was with Elton to go way back to his earlier material. He played this to me, singing along; he knew every word. Now it's *the* Whiley-Morton family anthem. Someone will put it on in the kitchen and then, one by one, we'll all drift into the room until we're all there, belting it out.

Billy Joel, 'Piano Man' – I'm a huge fan of Billy Joel. My Dad loved him, and I associate any Billy Joel song with Dad getting out the vinyl. But as with so many tracks I love, Steve first played this one to me. It was the story that drew me to it – a man in a bar who's seen it all.

Paul Robeson, 'Old Man River' – from the 1920s musical *Show Boat*. My God – what a voice! We went to see the musical when I was about eight and my Mum had lost a baby at birth. I remember there being a collective sense of 'What do we do now?' Someone had the brilliant idea of us all going to see a show. So there's a really poignant association for me; I think of Mum and Dad's courage when I hear the song. And, because it's about an old man looking death in the face, it reminds me of my grandfather, a great bear of a man, who I really loved.

Johnny Cash, 'Hurt' – his cover of the Nine-Inch Nails track. Watch the video and I defy you not to cry. His interpretation of the song is faultless, and made so poignant when you know that he died soon after recording it.

The Beatles, 'Hey Jude' – Because we named our son after it and because it's one of Steve's favourite songs.

Lee Marvin, 'Wandering Star' – I spent hours with my Grandad, watching old westerns, and our favourite was *Paint Your Wagon*. I had the seven-inch of this track, and the B-side was Clint Eastwood singing 'I Talk to the Trees'. When I went on Zane Lowe's show to take part in 'Versus', in which he pits himself against fellow DJs, my last song was 'Wandering Star', so I have actually managed to play it on Radio 1, and I have to say that it went down very well.

Dolly Parton, 'I Will Always Love You' – I spent a lot of time weighing up whether my favourite Dolly Parton track should be 'I Will Always Love You', 'Nine to Five' or 'Jolene'. She's one in a million, Dolly. I love her for the reasons that everyone does – for her brassy brilliance. But more than that – she has an amazing voice. In the end I decided on 'I Will Always Love You' as it's a song steeped in emotion – about love and letting go. Not only does she sing this better than anyone else, but Dolly actually wrote this herself. God this makes me weep.

Foo Fighters, 'Everlong' – This seems to keep coming up, but that's because I just adore it. It's one of those songs you hear and wish someone had written for you. I have had the privilege of hearing it sung live many times and it always gets better.

Massive Attack, 'Unfinished Sympathy' – one of Steve and my songs. I was working at the *Power Station* when it came out and so I was very focused on visuals and the video was groundbreaking, made in a single shot. I remember hearing them play this song as the sun went down at Phoenix Festival, a great musical moment. I was overjoyed when they played on my Channel 4 show a few years later.

Coldplay, 'Fix You' – When I listened to this for the first time, I liked it, but I didn't initially recognise its power. It was a slow-burner for me, but it's an extraordinary song, made all the more poignant when you understand that it is about loss. It's now one of my all-time favourite songs.

Green Day, 'Basketcase' – My anthem from the days of the Evening Session.

Arctic Monkeys, 'Mardy Bum' – Lyrics of genius, about a boy who loves his girl but not when she's being moody. Smacks of resignation and despair – I find it so poignant and it makes me wince and resolve never to be in a strop again. It's amazing because it was written by someone so young and yet so knowing.

Grandmaster Flash and the Furious Five, 'White Lines' – This was so groundbreaking when it came out, the beginning of rap and hip-hop; it was unlike anything I'd heard before and the subject matter was a million miles away from my world in a little village in the English Midlands.

Me

And that just leaves . . . me. I find it almost impossible to take a step back and describe myself. I suppose the best way, perhaps the only way for any of us to create an accurate self-portrait, is to look at the people around us who matter; they're the ones who've made us who we are, we're each the sum of all of our parts – friends, family, work colleagues.

There are three people who really helped me start out on my career. I've described my connection with John Peel elsewhere in this book. Suffice to say he was someone who I was in awe of, who became a great friend. One thing that made John special was that he never grew jaded; he never lost his enthusiasm and excitement at seeing a particular band and he never stopped being starstruck. Once when John and I were working at Glastonbury, Lonnie Donegan came by and played for us. I have to confess that I knew next to nothing about Lonnie Donegan, but John explained to me why he mattered. John could be incredibly moving and eloquent and he was almost in tears talking about Lonnie Donegan and how pivotal he had been in the 1960s. John couldn't quite believe he was going to meet the King of Skiffle and I felt humbled because I hadn't appreciated who we were about to see. Sure enough, when Lonnie Donegan arrived, John only managed to whisper, 'I am so privileged to meet you.'
   Alongside that worshipful love of music was an iconoclasm and anarchic streak that made John so rich and funny to have

around at Radio 1. The Radio 1 Christmas party is something of an institution, and I remember dreading them at first; I didn't know anyone and no one really talked to me. John was famous for misbehaving; he objected to the forced conviviality. I remember standing there talking to someone at the last Christmas party John was at, and he brushed past and gave me a swift pinch. I didn't quite know what to make of it. 'Oh my God,' I thought. 'John Peel has just pinched my arse.' But then a few months later I was listening to Moyles doing breakfast and he announced that John Peel had pinched his bottom at the Christmas party – if I conducted a survey I'd almost certainly discover that he had a go at everyone that night. I'd failed to feel the irony in the pinch.

Someone who took me under his wing and inspired me very early on was Scott Piering, an enigmatic character who promoted bands. I met him when I was working at Planet 24 on the ill-fated *Club X*. He was a quiet American who was responsible for the success of a number of bands in the early nineties. It's his voice doing the spoken lines in many of The KLF's tracks, including 'Justified and Ancient' and 'Last Train to Transcendental'. Scott was a father figure to me, and a tutor in the dark arts of the industry. I found him wise and kind and generous. He really helped me in many ways – not least by introducing me to everyone he knew.

Thinking back to those first heady days, when (largely because of Scott), I was hanging out with people from the music industry for the first time, I realise how naïve I was, but Scott never made me feel foolish. He took me up to Manchester to see a New Order gig, with a bunch of people, among them James Brown, who was then editor of *NME*. We saw the band play and I stood at the front of the crowd, watching bassist Peter Hook and thinking he was the sexiest thing I'd ever laid eyes on. After the gig we went to the infamous Haçienda club. Everyone I was with, except for James, disappeared *en masse* into the loos. I was so much less streetwise than they were and clearly all of them – except James and me – had taken an e. James and I are probably the only people who can claim to have been at the Haçienda without taking ecstasy. We were this hilarious pair of stiffs, chatting away about the gig, wondering out loud where the others had got to, thinking that perhaps it was time we called it a night.

Scott died tragically young, of cancer. At his funeral, the service finished and we began to file out of the crematorium, then someone hit the 'play' button and we heard Scott's voice for the final time. He had such style, right to the last.

The final person I'd describe as a mentor and who had a huge influence on me was Tony Wilson – Mr Manchester, as he was known. I got to know him indirectly through Scott Piering, who'd got me close to all things Factory – New Order, the Haçienda nightclub, the Happy Mondays. Tony also founded In the City, a music festival which discovered and promoted new bands. Each year the *Evening Session* would decamp up there and get involved in the festival, broadcasting from Madchester. Tony was a bombastic, formidable, magnificent man – always sharp-suited and sharp-tongued and with that wry smile on his face. He was responsible for encouraging and promoting so much of the music that I loved. I was always in awe of him and even slightly terrified. One of the finest compliments I've ever received was when I was watching a documentary about music TV and Tony Wilson pointed out that *The Word* was always held in high regard because of the bands that came on and played, and then went on to say that it had been me who'd booked them. It was like your dad patting you on the head when you'd had a good school report and saying, 'Well done.' High praise indeed.

It almost goes without saying that the people who've really mattered to me throughout my life, who've nurtured me, kept me grounded, made me the person I am, are my family – my grandparents, Mum and Dad, Steve and my lovely children.

My grandfather died eight years ago. He was a giant of a man; a classic patriarch. I have the most wonderful memories of him. He was a keen angler and he and I spent hours together fishing. There'd always be a tub of maggots in the fridge and sometimes eels in the bath. He tried his hand at absolutely everything, brewed his own beer, grew his own tomatoes – hour after hour he'd be out in that greenhouse – he even made jewellery. One of my happiest memories as a child was lying in the crook of his arm, resting on his stomach and watching westerns on TV. He bequeathed to me a love of Cowboys and Indians, fishing, Crown Green Bowling and Perry Como.

My mother is an incredible woman. Her life has involved real trauma, but she shows no self-pity, only compassion for others. She's always been a campaigner, someone who stands up for those who can't help themselves. When she perceived that there was the need for a social outlet for Frances and her friends, she set about putting something together for them, and the result was the Rocking Road Runner Club – Northampton's hugely successful nightclub for adults with learning disabilities. She doesn't see problems, she looks for solutions and somehow she always manages to pull things off. She never fails at anything she sets her mind to. When I was at school she used to organise fundraising barn dances that we all adored, in a proper barn, complete with hay bales, square dancing – the lot. Everything she embarks upon is done to perfection. She is principled and moral and along with my wonderful Dad, she's the bravest and most honest person I know.

My Dad is one of the kindest and most selfless people you could ever hope to meet – there is nothing he wouldn't do to help another person. When I was young he used to take me swimming training at 5 a.m. and pick me up from late-night parties in far-flung places – and all this while coping with Frances and working hard on the building sites. These days he gets up at the crack of dawn to come and look after my children who all think he's the best grandfather in the world. While I'm showering he'll make me a bacon sandwich and slip it into my bag to discover on the train. He's a legend in his local pub – where he provides entertainment every night. He's one of those people everybody likes, and he can share a joke with anyone from Chris from Coldplay or Sarah from Girls Aloud to the man who comes over to fix the dishwasher. He had a difficult childhood and he and Mum struggled through having Frances, but he's an optimist by nature and I can honestly say that I've never once heard him complain about anything.

My Dad's already decided on the song he wants played at his funeral – it's 'Always Look on the Bright Side of Life' and that perfectly sums him up – no matter what blows life has dealt him he will always bounce back with a smile on his face, a pint in his hand and a joke to tell. He's universally loved – in the pub (his second home), at the school gates (all the mums adore 'Grandad' and say his wisecracks make their day) and by all his mates, whether from the village or from the Saint's Rugby Club supporters (he's a regular).

He's all about making others feel good and putting a smile on people's faces – there is nothing he wouldn't do for someone else. What a testimony. How many people can you say that about? It makes me very proud to be his daughter and he means the world to me.

I find it very hard to talk about my feelings for Steve – much easier to set them down in print. We complement each other perfectly because we're complete opposites. I'm shy, quiet and hate confrontation; Steve is gregarious (loud), loves being the centre of attention and thrives on heated discussion and debate. We're still together after seventeen years, which suggests that we've mastered the art of the compromise. We're different in other ways, too. He hates showbiz and all the trappings of the celeb world, I love a bit of a starry bash and indulging in some celeb-spotting. He grounds me – without him I could see myself being sucked into a far more vacuous and shallow existence. He won't tolerate any of that rubbish. He's endlessly amusing though when it comes to his 'search for enlightenment' – self-help books, vitamin supplements and feng shui. The house is gradually filling up with Buddhas and dragons and bells that go tinkle in the night as he breaks down my resistance. If I was asked to sum Steve up in one word it'd be 'dynamic'. He has such a lust for life, always trying out new things, taking on new challenges and conquering them, from cooking to dog training to photography. In that way I think he reminds me of my beloved grandfather. There's nothing sexier than seeing your man bombing down a mountain at high speed on a snowboard or flying behind a boat on a wakeboard. There is no one in this life that I'd rather be on this journey with, never has been and never will be. He likes to say that he realised early on that he'd be fairly low down my list of priorities, when he suggested we elope and I said I couldn't leave my family behind. Back then it was just Mum, Dad and Frances he came behind, now there's also India, Jude, Cass, Coco and Boosh, the dog. It's nonsense, of course, he's my number one, but I'm eternally indebted to him for being my equal partner in juggling love and affection for the whole tribe – he's the most brilliant father and he's my best friend.

India would like to be the Nigella Lawson for the *Skins* generation and marry Alex Turner from the Arctic Monkeys and, were it not for the delightful Alexa Chung, I think both things would be possible. She's a great photographer and artist and applies make-up with the skill of a professional – I have no doubt she'll succeed in whatever she decides to do. Together we've learned to snowboard and wakeboard, sung our hearts out and sobbed to *Moulin Rouge*, lusted after Keith Murray from We Are Scientists, baked cupcakes, eaten chips and watched *The Graduate* in swanky hotels, attended every Harry Potter premiere and gig after gig after gig . . .

This year we've been on an extraordinary journey – from the day I found out I was pregnant, every step of the way, right up to the moment Coco was born. It's been hard for India, the whole balance of our relationship has shifted with the arrival of another child and I think she felt the loss of her position in the family as the only daughter. But she has been so brave and such a great help to me that I sometimes wonder who the child in our relationship is . . .

When I returned to work after having Coco, one thing that struck me was the number of times people said, 'Welcome Home.' It sums up for me so perfectly what it's like to work at Radio 1. It does feel like home. The team there are like family, and so are the listeners. I passionately love broadcasting and these days it feels like second nature to me, to the extent that I'd only been back behind my desk and on air for five minutes or so before I felt as though I'd never ever been away. I love the intimacy of it, the feeling of connection with the people who listen to the show, the thrill of discovering new bands.

If in twenty years' time I'm still on air introducing people to new music, like Annie Nightingale, Fluff Freeman, Johnny Walker and John Peel, each of whom made broadcasting their life's work, then I'll have succeeded in my life's dream. I love music and I love broadcasting and as long as I'm still able to combine the two I'll be happy.

Acknowledgements

With heartfelt thanks to my brilliant family for helping to join the dots in my sketchy recollections. When people ask 'How do you do it all?', the truth is 'I don't!'. I am completely indebted to you all for everything you do – especially you, Mum and Dad. Thanks also to my Radio 1 family and lifelong friends, to all the musicians who've ever crossed the threshold of the Live Lounge, to all at Virgin books, to Louisa, for your commitment and enthusiasm and to Margaret – with whom I shared a pregnancy and a birth. You are one patient, understanding and stylish lady, thank you. And to Steve, India, Jude, Cass and Coco – I promise that now the book's finished I'll start to cook you proper meals. No, really . . .